AN
**OWNERS
GUIDE**

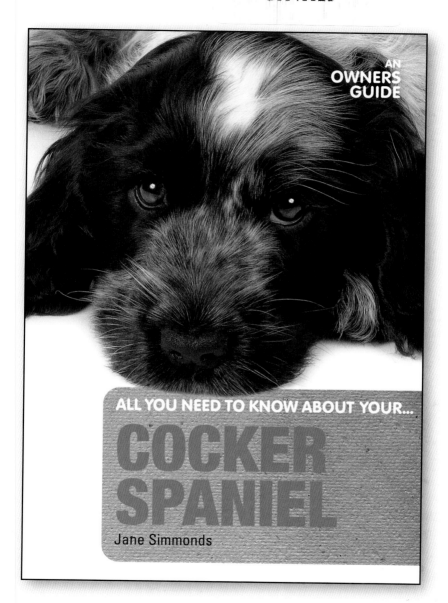

ALL YOU NEED TO KNOW ABOUT YOUR...

COCKER
SPANIEL

Jane Simmonds

Acknowledgements

The publishers would like to thank the following for help with photography: Jane Simmonds (Shenmore), Gill Moutrey (Sunzo), Alison Matthews (Sonham), Andy Fisher (Spinnchetti gundogs), Gareth Lawler (Roqfolly), Mary Braybrook, Geoff Brown, Hearing Dogs for Deaf People, and David Tomlinson (pages 12, 76, 100). page 79 © istockphoto.com/George Cairns.

Cover: Cockerbye Belle Colour owned by Rachel Appleby. Image © Tracy Morgan.

The question of gender

The 'he' pronoun is used throughout this book instead of the rather impersonal 'it', but no gender bias is intended.

© 2010 Pet Book Publishing Company Limited.

First published in 2010 by The Pet Book Publishing Company Limited
St. Martin's Farm, Zeals, Warminster, BA12 6NP.
Reprinted 2011, 2012, 2014.

ISBN

978-1-906305-29-1
1-906305-29-3

Printed and bound in China through Printworks International Ltd.

Contents

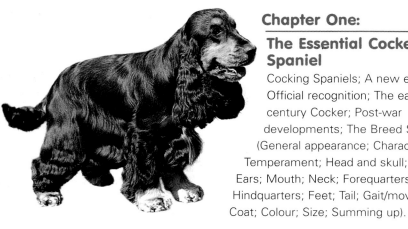

The Essential Cocker Spaniel

The Cocker Spaniel is one of the British spaniel breeds included within the Kennel Club Gundog group. Other spaniel breeds with a shared heritage include the American Cocker, Clumber Spaniel, English Springer, Welsh Springer, Field Spaniel and Sussex Spaniel.

Spaniel-type dogs were known to exist in this country many centuries ago. Geoffrey Chaucer refers to a "spaynel" (the Middle English spelling of spaniel) in *The Wife of Bath's Prologue*, which is part of the great medieval poem *The Canterbury Tales*, written in the 14th century.

The Cocker was highly prized as a working gundog, flushing out game.

SPANIEL ORIGINS

It is often said that spaniels originated from Spain ('spaniel' being a corruption of the French word 'espagnol', meaning Spanish). This theory is based on sources such as the oldest English book on hunting, *Master of Game* (1406-1413) written by Edward Plantagenet, Duke of York, who wrote of spaniels that "their nature cometh from Spain". Although there is no real evidence to support this claim, it remains a popular theory today.

It is known that these early spaniels were sporting dogs, used in the hunting of wild fowl and falconry – helping to flush quarry into the hunting nets or towards trained birds of prey. Dr Caius, a famed Elizabethan physician, describes these hunting spaniels in his *Treatise of Englishe Dogges* (translated from Latin in 1576), which was the earliest known attempt at a complete classification of dogs. He noted that the land spaniels were used for, "The Falcon, The Phesant, The Partridge and such like".

COCKING SPANIELS

Although spaniels had been used for centuries for sporting purposes, it was not until the 1800s that the Cocker or Cocking Spaniel emerged as a separate, distinct type. The name derives from the use of small spaniels for woodcock shooting, which had become popular at the time. These 'cocking' spaniels could get into the thickest undergrowth and flush out the woodcock to the waiting guns.

One of the first mentions of cocking spaniels in literature can be found in *The Sportsman's Cabinet* written by William Taplin in 1803. Taplin records that there were two types of spaniel at that time: the larger Springing Spaniel (forerunner of the modern Springer Spaniel), which was used on all kinds of game, and the smaller Cocker or Cocking Spaniel, which was used for woodcock shooting "to which they are more particularly appropriated and by nature seem designed."

He describes the Cocker as having "a shorter, more compact form, a

A New Era: Official

The Victorian era saw rapid advances in selective dog breeding and formal record keeping with the founding of the Kennel Club in 1873. Dog exhibiting was also developed at this time with the first organised dog show taking place in 1859. Formal Field Trials also began to be organised with the first one specifically for spaniels being won by a Cocker named Stylish Pride in 1899.

In early Kennel Club stud books, there was no separate classification of the Cocker Spaniel, despite the breed's long history. Instead Field Spaniels were divided into "Over 25 lbs" and "Under 25 lbs" with Cockers included in this latter category. This did not change until 1893 when the Kennel Club finally recognised the Cocker Spaniel as a separate breed but still retained the weight limit of 25 lbs. Up to this time, it was not unusual for Cockers and Field

rounder head, shorter nose, ears long (and the longer, the more admired), the limbs short and strong, the coat more inclined to curl than the springers…"

Colours were liver and white, red, red and white, black and white, solid liver "and not infrequently black with tanned legs and muzzle." This confirms black and tan as one of the oldest Cocker colours.

In the later part of the 19th century, it seems that different strains of Cocker Spaniel had been developed in different parts of the country, such as the Welsh Cocker (later to become the Welsh Springer) and the Devon Cocker. Stonehenge, the Victorian author, wrote in *The Dog in Health and Disease* (1859) that it was difficult to describe the Cocker in detail because there were so many regional variations, but generally he could be said to be "a light active spaniel of about 14 lbs weight on the average, sometimes reaching 20 lbs, with very elegant shapes, and a lively and spirited carriage."

Recognition

Spaniels to be born in the same litter and be entered in different classes at shows, depending on how much they weighed.

Cocker enthusiasts were deeply opposed to the arbitrary weight limit of 25 lbs being imposed by the Kennel Club, arguing that type was far more important than weight. Not surprisingly, the breed made little progress during this time with the Field Spaniel being by far the more popular breed – a situation that is reversed today. Eventually the Kennel Club removed the weight limit in 1901.

A year later, the Cocker Spaniel Club was formed and a Breed Standard was drawn up by a committee composed mainly of shooting men. Although the Standard has been amended slightly over subsequent decades, it remains the same in essence today as it was when it was first produced.

Four pre-War "Of Ware" Cockers (artist unknown). The dogs left to right are Ch. Benet of Ware, Exquisite Model of Ware, Sir Galahad of Ware and Australian Ch. Silver Templa of Ware.

THE EARLY 20TH CENTURY COCKER

From the early 1900s, the Cocker Spaniel went from strength to strength, gaining in popularity year by year. In 1914, there were just 400 Cockers registered with the Kennel Club, but, by 1947, this had risen to a peak figure of 27,000. Today's registrations have stabilised at about 10,000 to 12,000 a year.

During this time, the breed evolved in type quite markedly. It is generally accepted that the forerunner of the modern Cocker was James Farrow's Ch. Obo, born in 1879. At this time, Cockers were quite different in size and proportions to today's Cocker, as can be demonstrated by Obo's vital statistics. He weighed 22 lbs, was only 10 inches high, and measured 29 inches from nose to tail, so we can see that he was quite a small dog, long in body and quite low to the ground. Colours most often seen at this time were solid liver, liver and tan, solid black, black and tan.

The fashion for long, low dogs continued for some time, but eventually a taller, more symmetrical Cocker evolved during the first part of the 20th century. This was largely due to the influence of the early Cocker pioneers, such as Mr C.A. Phillips (Rivington), R. De Courcy Peele (Bowdler) and Mr Richard Lloyd, who used outcrosses to Field

The legendary Ch. Obo (right) pictured with his sire, Fred.

Exquisite Model of Ware: Winner of Crufts Best in Show in 1938 and 1939.

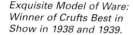

Spaniels, Springer Spaniels and English Setters to increase size. More colours also began to be seen, including blue roan and solid red; the latter due to judicious imports from North America. Mention must also be made of H.S. Lloyd, who inherited his father's (Richard Lloyd) kennel in 1906 and founded the world famous Of Ware line of Cockers, which continues today in the ownership of his daughter, Jennifer Lloyd-Carey. The Of Ware dogs had an enormous influence on the breed's development, and Mr Lloyd's record of six Best in Show wins at Crufts with three different Cockers is unlikely ever to be surpassed.

POST-WAR DEVELOPMENTS

In the early years of the Cocker as an officially recognised breed, it was very much a dual-purpose dog.

There is now a definite split between Cockers bred from show lines and those used as working dogs.

Breeders worked their dogs in the field as well as showed them. In 1909, the Kennel Club introduced a requirement that, to become a Champion in the show ring, a Cocker would also have to gain a qualifying certificate to demonstrate working abilities and, for some years, this no doubt helped to retain the Cocker as a breed that could work and show.

However, by 1958, it was found that few exhibitors were bothering to gain the working certificate and so the Kennel Club introduced the intermediate title of Show Champion, retaining the title of Champion for those dogs who did gain the working certificate. The title of Dual Champion also exists for those that become both Field Trial Champions and Show Champions. While there have been a handful of Show Champion Cockers who have gained their working certificates and become full Champions, there has never been a Dual Champion Cocker in modern times.

These changes marked the development of the two different strains of Cocker that exist today: the show-type Cocker and the working-type Cocker, generally referred to as the Working Cocker.

POINTS OF ANATOMY

Occiput
Skull
Nape
Crest
Stop
Chest
Withers
Loin
Croup
Flews
Tail
Muzzle
Shoulder
Stifle
Foreleg
Lower thigh
Wrist
Hock
Front foot
Flank
Hind foot
Elbow
Dewclaw
Stopper pad
Pastern

This split was inevitable once breeders started breeding for different purposes with show breeders concentrating on conformation and the Breed Standard, and working breeders concentrating on working ability only. The development of separate strains has resulted in differences in physical appearance – the glamorous show dog versus the functional working dog. There are also some differences in character, with show-bred dogs having a lower hunting drive than working dogs.

THE BREED STANDARD

Like every breed recognised by the Kennel Club in the UK, the Cocker has a written Breed Standard that describes the ideal characteristics, temperament and physical appearance of the breed. Dogs entered at shows are judged against this Standard, but it is important to stress that Breed Standards do not just describe the perfect show dog. The Cocker Standard was originally drawn up by men who worked their dogs, and while there have been some minor amendments, the Standard still retains the original emphasis on a dog that is fit for his original function as a sporting dog.

General Appearance

The Cocker is a compact, sturdy dog, free from exaggerations. He is sometimes described as being "cobby", using equine terminology for a short-backed, stocky, little horse. He is well-balanced, measuring about the same from the top of the shoulder blades (the withers) to the floor as from the same point to the base of his tail. However, in practice many modern show dogs are slightly shorter in the body than the Standard describes.

Characteristics

The Cocker has a merry nature with a constantly wagging tail. He has a busy, bustling movement, particularly when following a scent, and will happily force his way through the thickest cover. Although the bustling movement is perhaps more obvious in a working dog, even the owner of a pet Cocker will recognise this description as they watch their dog eagerly following his nose into the nearest available undergrowth!

Temperament

The Cocker is happy and extrovert – a subdued, timid personality is definitely alien for the breed. He has

The merry Cocker is a happy, bustling breed, with an ever-wagging tail.

a kind, gentle temperament and is very affectionate, often greeting complete strangers as if they were long-lost friends. He expects his affection to be reciprocated by all he meets and can be confused when this is not always forthcoming!

He is also energetic and enthusiastic. "Life is for living" could be his motto, as he likes to be on the go, wanting to get involved in everything his family is doing.

Head and skull
The Cocker has a balanced head with the skull about the same length as the foreface (the stop is the indentation between the eyes). The muzzle needs to be square not snipey (weak and pointed) to give sufficient strength to the lower jaw. The skull is slightly domed but

The Cocker has a balanced head, with a slightly domed skull.

not in an exaggerated way; round, apple heads are not desirable. The head should not be too broad, although wide, white markings on the head of a particoloured dog can give the optical illusion of an over-broad skull when this is not actually the case.

The Cocker needs a good-sized nose with wide, open nostrils to help him perform his function as a working dog, sniffing out fallen game.

Eyes
The eyes should be full and slightly oval in shape, not too large or prominent in any way. Large, prominent eyes would be more prone to injury in the field. The rims should be tight, because loose bottom lids would hinder a working dog, making the eyes more susceptible to infection or injury when the dog is working. However, some Cockers have unpigmented (pink instead of brown) third eyelids.

The long ears of a Cocker should reach to the tip of the nose.

permitted. This is because the liver colour gene has a fading effect on eye colour, making it impossible for dark-brown eyes to be produced – although the greeny/yellow eyes seen on some liver dogs are not desirable.

A Cocker can use his eyes to look sad and doleful on occasion (as any owner knows), but, in general, the Cocker has a sweet, gentle expression and his eyes reflect his intelligence and his cheerful, good nature.

Ears

The Cocker is well known for his long, pendulous ears, which are set on level with the eyes. The ear flaps (leathers) should extend to the tip of the nose. Cocker ears, particularly on show dogs, can look longer than they are, as the hair on a mature dog's ear can often grow inches longer than the length of the actual leathers. This is why a pet Cocker whose hair has been clipped short – as some owners prefer– can look as if he has much shorter ears than a dog in full show coat.

These should not be confused with loose bottom lids. Unpigmented third eyelids can look more obvious when a dog also has loose bottom lids, but they are not mentioned in the Standard as a fault and they are not a health issue for the dog.

Eyes should be dark brown or brown, except for liver-coloured dogs (solids and particolours) where a lighter shade of brown (hazel) is

Mouth

As a gundog breed expected to be able to carry quite heavy game for some distance without damaging it, it is important for a Cocker to have good, strong jaws and the correct scissor bite. Show judges often place great importance on correct bites, because a faulty bite is very difficult to breed out and would also prevent the dog from carrying out his original working function.

Undershot (where the lower jaw extends beyond the upper jaw) and overshot (where the top jaw extends beyond the lower jaw) bites are sometimes seen in the breed and while they are considered faults for a show or working dog, they usually have little impact on the life of a pet dog. However, such dogs should obviously not be bred from.

Neck

The neck should be moderate in length and muscular. A Cocker needs to have strong neck muscles to be able to lift and carry game, but the neck must not be too long or too short. Too long a neck makes the dog look unbalanced and exaggerated; too short a neck is usually associated with poor shoulder angulation and makes the dog look very 'stuffy'. The neck should join the body smoothly with no lumps and bumps where it meets the shoulders, and there should be no excess loose skin on the throat.

Forequarters

The dog's shoulder assembly is made up of the shoulder blade and the upper arm. These bones should be "well laid back", meaning they slope backwards and ideally form close to a right angle where they meet. Well-laid-back shoulders give a

The body is short and square with a firm, straight topline.

good reach of neck, sufficient width to the body, and the long, economical stride essential for a sporting dog with the stamina to work all day.

Steep shoulders and short, straight upper arms produce a dog with a short neck and a narrow front, which results in stilted, choppy movement. Such a dog would tire more easily and not be able to cover as much ground as a dog with well-angulated shoulders.

A Cocker also needs to have strong, straight, well-boned legs. As a small breed originally intended to work through thick cover (undergrowth), long legs are not required. But the legs should not be too short and stumpy, as this would affect the dog's ability to work, as well as giving an unbalanced appearance.

Body

The Cocker has a short, square body with well-rounded ribs, giving plenty of room for the heart and lungs. The depth of body is about the same as the length of leg. The rib cage is deep and should go right down to the elbow and extend as far back as the loins. The muscular area between the end of the ribs and the hindquarters (the couplings) needs to be short and strong, as this area helps power the hindquarters.

The topline (meaning the line of

Hindquarters

A Cocker should have broad, well-muscled thighs and a well-bent stifle to give him the strength and power needed to do his job of work, thrusting under thick cover etc. A well-bent stifle is produced when the upper and lower thigh bones are a good length and are laid back at a sufficient angle where they meet at the stifle joint. Good angulation here produces a hock joint that is relatively low to the ground, allowing the dog to drive well from behind.

Straight stifles, without the necessary bend, result in stilted movement, lacking drive. However, too much angulation is not desirable, as this produces exaggerated 'long' stifles, which can result in unsound movement.

the back) should be firm and straight, only starting to slope gently from the end of the loin down to where the tail starts, contributing to the rounded rump the Cocker is known for.

Feet

A Cocker needs round, well-cushioned, tight feet to protect him when he is working; thin, flat feet with spreading toes are not desirable, as they are more prone to injury and will offer little in the way of cushioning to support the dog's body on a long day in the field.

Tail

The Cocker is famous for his ever-wagging tail and is known worldwide as the 'merry Cocker'.

Originally, the Cocker was a traditionally docked breed, with a portion of the tail removed after birth in order to prevent tail injuries when working. However, since April 2006, tail docking has been banned completely in Scotland and is only

Traditionally, the tail was docked.

Now all Cockers have full tails unless they are working gundogs.

permitted in England and Wales for Cockers (and certain other working breeds) where there is evidence that the dog is intended for working.

The practical result of this change in the law is that most show-type puppies and puppies bred purely as family pets are now left undocked and the only docked puppies should come from breeders who work their dogs and can prove that their puppies are likely to be used for working.

The tail is set on just below the level of the back, but not too low, and is carried level with the back. Sometimes when excited, the tail is carried higher, particularly noticeable in a male. The undocked tail is well feathered, slightly curved, and ideally should not extend beyond the dog's hock joint (an overlong tail can give an unbalanced appearance). The docked tail should not be too long or too short to interfere with the Cocker's enthusiastic tail action when working. Working breeders still legally able to have their puppies docked generally opt for a relatively long dock where just the last third of the tail is removed.

Gait/Movement

The Cocker is a sound, free-moving dog, with the front and back legs moving parallel in a straight line, turning neither in nor out. As mentioned before, good angulation in the forehand (shoulder) and hindquarters means he can use long strides to cover the ground well, which is so important in a working dog.

The Cocker covers the ground easily in long strides.

The glamorous coat of a show Cocker would be impractical for a working dog.

Colour

The Standard describes Cocker coat colours as "various" but does not lay down a list of permitted colours. The only rule is that no white can appear on a solid colour except on the chest. This is really only relevant for the show ring, as white markings elsewhere on a mostly solid-coloured dog is of no real importance for a pet Cocker or a working dog.

The Cocker probably has more coat colour variations than any other breed, although some colours are more commonly seen than others. Solid colours include black, red, golden, liver (now called chocolate by some breeders), black and tan, and liver and tan. The particolours include the roans where the coloured hair is mixed with white hair to give a mottled appearance. There is blue roan, orange/lemon roan and liver/chocolate roan. The roans may also have tan markings, such as blue roan and tan, or liver roan and tan. There are also the "and whites" (where the background colour of the

The Cocker's Coat

A Cocker should have a close-fitting, flat, silky coat on his body with feathering on his legs and underneath his body. The feathering not only looks attractive but helps to protect the body from injury when working. The coat should not be "too profuse", as a very long, thick coat would get caught up in the undergrowth and be a positive hindrance to a working dog.

Many modern show Cockers do grow very thick coats with long feathering, which looks very glamorous when presented correctly but would be quite impracticable for a working dog. Dogs bred from working lines tend to have much sparser coats for this reason.

coat is pure white with no roaning), such as black and white, orange and white, liver/chocolate and white. These colours may also have tan markings; the tricolours, such as black, white and tan and liver/chocolate and tan. Where the "and white" coats show some visible ticking (small flecks of colour on the white background), they are referred to as "and white ticked" e.g. black and white ticked.

In recent years, the sable colouring has become more popular. Sable refers to a basically black (or liver dog) where tan markings have spread extensively underneath the coat, mixing with the black (or liver) hairs. Sable particolours are also possible. Sable is somewhat controversial; some breeders feel it is not a traditional Cocker colour, but it has probably existed for many years and is perfectly acceptable according to the Breed Standard.

Cocker Colours: Solid Colours

Black.

Golden.

Black and tan.

Liver, also known as chocolate.

Cocker Colours: Parti colours

Blue roan.

Orange and white.

Tricolour: Black and white with tan markings.

Size

For male Cockers, the desired height is approximately 39-41 cms (15$\frac{1}{2}$-16 ins); for bitches it is approximately 38-39 cms (15-15$\frac{1}{2}$ ins). Weight is approximately: 13-14.5 kgs (28-32 lbs).

So a Cocker dog should be a little bigger and heavier than a Cocker bitch, but note that the weights and heights given are approximate only (the lessons have been learned from the old days when Cockers were given an arbitrary weight limit that had to be complied with). The Cocker is essentially a 'big dog in a small package', but his weight should come from his sturdy bone and muscular body – he should never be fat or flabby.

SUMMING UP

The Cocker Spaniel has come a long way since the breed was first developed as a purely working dog in the 19th century. Nowadays, this is a truly versatile breed with worldwide popularity as a family pet and show dog. But the Cocker's sporting roots have not been forgotten. Working Cockers have become increasingly popular in recent years and have a dedicated following, whether this be for the demands of competitive Field Trials or as weekend shooting companions.

The breed's trainability and natural instincts have also been put to good use in various services for the community. Working Cockers have been successfully trained as detection (sniffer) dogs for the security services and Customs and Excise. Cockers of both types work as assistance dogs for deaf or disabled people, and volunteer as therapy dogs, visiting homes for the elderly, hospices and hospitals.

Although Cockers have certainly changed over the years, most noticeably the development into two distinct strains, some things remain the same. Whether show- or working-type, a Cocker is still the same small, sturdy dog with a big personality, always ready to throw himself enthusiastically into everything life has to offer!

The versatile Cocker has proved valuable as an assistance dog, helping those with hearing disabilities.

Choosing A Cocker

Before you make any definite arrangements to buy a Cocker puppy, or adopt an older dog, it is a good idea to sit down and think about all the pros and cons, since owning a dog is a lifetime commitment and should never be taken lightly.

Probably the first thing to consider is whether a Cocker really is suitable for your family's lifestyle. Most people fall for the Cocker because of his attractive looks, his famous "merry" temperament and his compact size – being not too big but not too small either – but some fail to realise that this is no lap dog!

The Cocker is a busy, energetic dog that thrives on human company and likes to be involved with every family activity, no matter how mundane. This is not a breed that should be left alone for hours on end while you are at work. He needs plenty of exercise, not just a quick walk round the block once or twice a day. You also need to remember that this is a longhaired breed that needs regular grooming and will shed hair (some more than others); he may not be the dog for you if you are exceptionally house proud.

SHOW OR WORKING?

It is important to understand the differences between the two distinct Cocker strains – show-type and working – so that you can make the right choice for your family and lifestyle. Show-type dogs will be instantly recognisable to most people, having the typical domed head, long ears and glamorous coat with abundant feathering. As the name suggests, this is the type of Cocker seen at shows where dogs are judged against the Kennel Club Breed Standard. However, it is important to realise that many commercial breeders produce show-type Cockers. But 'show-type' does not mean that the breeder shows their dogs or that their puppies will be show quality; it simply means that they resemble this general type to a greater or lesser degree. Show-type dogs have been popular as family pets for many years, although their long feathering means that regular grooming and trimming are needed to keep the coat neat and tidy. Would-be owners also need to

Cockers from show lines retain working instincts, such as the ability to retrieve, but they may not have the speed and energy of dogs bred from working lines.

realise that just because a Cocker comes from show lines does not mean he has lost all the characteristics of a working gundog. Many show-type dogs like to pick up and carry items around. They will also use their noses to hunt through undergrowth like their working ancestors, although perhaps without the speed of today's purpose-bred Working Cockers. Although few show-type Cockers today do the job that they were originally bred for, there are still a handful of dedicated owners who work their show dogs to demonstrate that they have not lost their working abilities.

The working Cocker is becoming popular as a pet, but this type needs plenty of exercise and mental stimulation.

Working Cockers have become increasingly popular in recent years and are no longer confined to working homes as once was the case. Dogs are bred primarily for their working ability with less importance placed on conformation to the official Breed Standard. This means that a Working Cocker can look somewhat different to his show-type cousin. His skull is usually flatter and broader, without the slight dome of a show dog. His ears are shorter and his body often appears longer and leggier than a show dog. There is quite a variation in size from very large to quite small, so it is not possible to say that Working Cockers are always bigger or smaller than show-type dogs.

A working-type dog usually carries far less coat than a show dog, although there is, again, some variation, as some have thicker coats than others. This lack of coat means that a Working Cocker can appeal to owners who do not want to do much grooming, but there needs to be a clear understanding that there is a lot more to a Working Cocker than a short coat! As he was bred to work, he will usually have the kind of speed and stamina to enable him to work in the field all day. While it is unfair to generalise too much, it is true to say that many Working Cockers are far

Cockers have their own individual personalities, and whether you choose a male (left) or a female (right) comes down to personal preference.

more energetic than show-type Cockers; some can be on the go all day and still be up for more at the end of it! Mental stimulation is very important for this kind of dog; they need something to do to keep their minds and bodies occupied and they do best in a home where the owner provides the opportunity for activities such as canine agility or gundog training. They can and do make very good pets for the active family, but if you are a first-time dog owner with no experience of training an active working dog, a Working Cocker may not be the best choice for you.

MALE OR FEMALE?

A male Cocker is usually slightly bigger and heavier than a female, but there is very little difference in temperament between the two sexes and both make equally good family pets. Some say that bitches are easier to train and more affectionate. However, there is little evidence for this in Cockers and the theory is perhaps based on the bigger, guarding breeds. In reality, all Cockers have their own individual personalities, which are influenced less by gender and more by other factors such as genetics, socialisation and training.

Health Issues

Although Cockers are generally robust dogs, often living well into their teens, there are a few hereditary health conditions that sometimes occur. You need to be aware of these, and the screening tests available, to ensure that the breeders you contact have done everything possible to avoid hereditary problems in their dogs. See Chapter Six for further information.

These are the most significant hereditary problems known in Cockers:

EYES

There are a number of eye conditions seen in Cockers, which include GPRA (generalised progressive retinal atrophy) and CPRA (centralised progressive retinal atrophy) – diseases that affect the retinas, causing blindness – and glaucoma. All Cockers used for breeding should be annually eye-tested for the first two conditions, and tested once for predisposition to glaucoma (gonioscopy test). The eye test is limited, because it cannot detect carriers of the disease, nor can it tell whether a dog will go on to develop the disease in later life. Fortunately, breeders now have available a DNA test for the form of GPRA (offered by the American company, Optigen), which can identify a tested dog as: clear, carrier or affected. As long as at least one parent is DNA tested as clear,

There are certain practical considerations that might influence your choice of a male or a female. Bitches come into season once or twice a year (depending on their cycle) from the age of six months onwards. During seasons, it is the owner's responsibility to keep their bitch safe from the attentions of entire male dogs. This means that exercise may have to be limited or confined to on-lead walks in areas where there are no other dogs around. During and after seasons, a bitch may also be affected by behavioural changes, such as moodiness, due to the fluctuating hormone levels. There may also be a breeders can ensure that no affected puppies are produced. Annual eye-testing should also be continued, as the Optigen test only tests for one eye condition.

KIDNEYS

There is a kidney disease that affects Cockers under the age of two, which is commonly known as familial nephropathy (FN). This condition is not common but it is always fatal. A new DNA test has now been developed for this disease, which identifies dogs as clear/normal, carriers or affected. Affected dogs are produced when two carriers are unknowingly mated together. However, the advent of the DNA test means that this can now be avoided; breeders using the test can guarantee that none of their puppies will develop this condition.

HIP DYSPLASIA

There is evidence of some hip dysplasia in the breed, but as only a relatively small number of dogs have been hip scored, it is difficult to know the true extent of the problem. As more breeders submit their dogs for scoring, it will be possible to get a more accurate picture. The current breed average is 14, meaning that breeders should aim to breed from dogs where the score for each hip adds up to below this figure. Each hip is scored from a perfect 0 to a worst possible score of 53.

lapse in house-training, as in-season bitches tend to urinate more than normal.

Spaying a bitch will, of course, mean the end to her seasons and any of these issues, as well as having other health benefits. But note that some vets prefer not to spay until a bitch has had at least one season.

Many potential new owners are put off having a male because of fears that male dogs are difficult to let off the lead to exercise and will stray constantly, looking for the nearest bitch. In reality, both sexes will need persistent recall training, as their natural gundog instincts can make them 'selectively deaf' to the calls of their owner, especially when they are following a particularly interesting scent. Males can certainly be distracted by bitches, but generally only when there is a bitch in season in close proximity. A male can, of course, be neutered to reduce any excessive interest in the opposite sex, but neutering will not cure a dog with a poor recall – only training can do this.

MORE THAN ONE?

Some people make the mistake of thinking it is better to have two puppies at the same time because they will be able to keep each other company, especially if the owner works long hours and feels guilty about leaving a dog alone. This is probably the worst reason to take on two pups, as two puppies left alone for long periods will inevitably entertain themselves in whatever way they can, including barking and destructive behaviour. If you work long hours, it is not impossible to have a dog or dogs, but proper arrangements need to be made for care during the day, such as a dog crèche or a dog walker.

There is another potential problem that could arise, particularly if both puppies are the same sex. Same-sex puppies may appear to get along very well at first, but it is not unusual for their relationship to deteriorate as they reach adolescence, resulting in squabbles and, in serious cases, major fights. Even if the puppies are from different litters, this rivalry can still develop, particularly where their personalities are very similar. It is sometimes possible for such situations to improve as time goes by, but in some cases, there is no option but to separate the dogs permanently by finding a new home

Cockers are very collectable – but resist the temptation of taking home two puppies from the same litter.

for one of them – a heartbreaking decision for any owner.

There is also the risk that two puppies bought at the same time can bond too closely with each other, especially if they are allowed to spend all their time together.

This close bonding can lead to the puppies becoming too dependant on each other so that they are unable to cope with separation – even when this is necessary because of one puppy needing veterinary treatment, for example. This close relationship also means the puppies do not bond so well with their human family and can be slower to respond to training, preferring to play with each other rather than listen to their owner!

If you are a first-time owner without previous puppy training experience, it is better to start with one puppy that you can then devote all your attention to. You should never underestimate how demanding training just one puppy can be. You could then add to your canine family later, once your first Cocker is fully mature and well trained, which will not usually be before the age of 18 months.

EXERCISE REQUIREMENTS

How much exercise a Cocker needs will depend on his age and also, to some extent, on whether he comes from show or working lines.

While young puppies (of both types) will only need short walks to begin with, a mature Cocker needs sufficient daily exercise to keep his mind and body healthy and happy. A Cocker that is not given enough exercise of the right kind can suffer from health problems, such as obesity, or behavioural issues brought about by boredom and frustration. A fit, healthy Cocker will enjoy as much exercise as you can give him, but this

A Cocker will thrive on being given a variety of walks with different sights and smells.

Do not be impatient - it may take time to track down the puppy you want.

does not mean that he needs a 10-mile hike every day. Many show-type dogs will be happy with two good 30- to 40-minute walks a day, plus access to the garden at regular intervals for play/training sessions. However, many Working Cockers will need considerably more exercise than this, perhaps up to three hours a day, depending on their age and fitness levels.

Cockers of both types need an opportunity to use their brains and natural instincts when being exercised. A Cocker needs some variety and will get bored of going on the same walk every day. He will also need access to open areas where he can be let off the lead. Pavement walking on a lead does not offer a dog anywhere near as much exercise or mental stimulation as a walk that includes the opportunity for free-running in a field or park.

FINDING A COCKER PUPPY
The popularity of the Cocker has meant that many puppies are bred by breeders who are only interested in making money at the expense of the health and welfare of their dogs. Often people looking for a Cocker puppy make the mistake of thinking that as they want their dog to be "just

a pet", it does not matter too much where their pup comes from. Nothing could be further from the truth. If you are looking for a pet Cocker puppy, health and temperament should be very important priorities. No family wants a puppy with a poor temperament or one which suffers from a preventable hereditary disease. Responsible breeders always breed for good temperament, and should also use the available health-testing schemes to ensure their pups grow up to be as healthy as possible.

Here are some pointers to bear in mind in your search for a breeder:
• Go to a specialist breeder, not one that constantly advertises large numbers of popular breeds for sale. A specialist breeder will often only own Cockers, although some do also own one or two other breeds, and will have the knowledge and experience to discuss every aspect of the breed with potential buyers. Specialist breeders are usually members of at least one breed club (such as the Cocker Spaniel Club) and will usually be involved in activities with their dogs besides breeding, such as showing, working/field trials or agility.
• Always see a litter of puppies with their mother and as many other of the breeder's dogs as possible. This

It is important to see the mother with her puppies to get an idea of the temperament they are likely to inherit.

will allow you to see for yourself that they have good temperaments and are happy to meet visitors. Never buy from a pet shop or dealer where puppies are bought in from other premises – usually puppy farms – to be sold to whoever has the cash to pay for them

* Expect to be asked as many questions by the breeder as you ask him/her. Good breeders will always want to know as much about potential buyers as possible to ensure that the home offered is right for one of their puppies. Any breeder who asks no questions of potential buyers does not care about their puppies and is unlikely to be interested in offering any help or advice after a sale is made.

• Always check whether the parents of a litter have had the recommended health-screening tests, and ask to see the relevant certificates. Avoid any breeder who says that his/her dogs do not need any tests, as this demonstrates either that a breeder who does not care, or that they lack the necessary knowledge.

• Check whether the litter is Kennel Club registered. All good breeders will register their puppies with the KC rather than alternative commercial registries, but note that this is just a starting point. KC registration does not guarantee that a breeder is reputable; you should still be prepared to carry out your own checks. This applies to the KC Accredited Breeder Scheme, too. Membership of this scheme involves agreeing to comply with certain basic standards of good practice (including some health testing), but does not indicate that a breeder has necessarily been vetted or proven to be a good breeder.

• Ask whether the breeder will be willing to help you with advice after you have brought your puppy home. Good breeders will always be willing to offer after-sales support, and many will provide a sales contract that explains this in more detail, including a commitment to take back any of their puppies for rehoming, should this ever become necessary.

• Be patient! Good breeders do not have litters constantly available for sale, and many may have a waiting list for their puppies. Mistakes are often made by buyers who want a puppy now as they rush out and buy from the first litter they find, without doing any research or asking any questions. Remember, you will hopefully have your Cocker for many years so a wait of a few weeks or even months is nothing compared to this.

The puppies in the litter should be evenly matched and kept in a clean, fresh smelling environment.

- Never be tempted to buy a puppy because you feel sorry for it. It is understandable that some people may feel they are "rescuing" a puppy if they find a litter being reared in poor conditions or showing signs of ill health or with shy temperaments. Unfortunately, this just helps bad breeders stay in business, as more puppies will soon be born to replace the one just sold.
- Be very cautious of litters advertised in newspapers or on puppy sale websites on the internet. Although a few good breeders do use these mediums to advertise, they are also widely used by commercial breeders and puppy farmers. The best sources of information on reputable breeders are the Cocker Spaniel breed clubs. There are a large number of regional clubs as well as the parent club, the Cocker Spaniel Club. The Kennel Club also has details of breeders with litters available – but remember to do your own vetting on such breeders, as mentioned above.

VIEWING PUPPIES

Once the breeder you have chosen has a litter available, you will normally be invited to view the litter, but note that many responsible breeders will not allow visitors to see their puppies until they are over three or four weeks old. This is due to the risk of infection being brought in and also because a new Cocker mum usually needs peace and quiet

A healthy puppy has a sturdy, well-rounded body and a soft, silky coat.

to concentrate on the hard work of looking after her puppies. Once the pups are old enough to receive visitors, breeders will often encourage you to visit several times until the puppies are ready to leave for their new homes at eight weeks old. This gives you plenty of time to get to know the breeder and their dogs, and to ask questions.

If you have young children, it is often better to visit the first time without the children. This makes it easier if you decide that there is something about the breeder or the litter you do not feel comfortable with. It is much harder to walk away, despite your misgivings, if your children have already seen the puppies and fallen in love with them.

When viewing a litter for the first time, there are several things you should be looking out for:

- Are the conditions where the puppies are living clean? As puppies need to toilet frequently, it is impossible to avoid a little odour sometimes, but there should be no overpowering smell and bedding should be clean and recently washed. Water bowls should be clean and contain fresh water.

- Do the puppies look healthy and happy? Healthy, well-reared pups will have sturdy, well-rounded bodies – not skinny but not too fat either – and will have clear eyes and sweet-smelling ears with no sign of discharge. Their coats will be soft and silky to the touch and there should be no sign of scurfy, itchy skin. Once at the active stage, puppies should greet visitors enthusiastically and not hide away to avoid contact, which would indicate a shy temperament.

- Is mum happy to meet visitors? The mother of a newborn litter may be suspicious of strangers, out of concern for her pups, but once the litter is less dependent and the weaning process has begun, she should be happy to meet visitors and allow them to handle her puppies.

- Is the litter housed indoors or outdoors? If puppies are reared indoors, they often receive more attention from the breeder and other family members and also get used to the sights and sounds of a normal household. This will help them adapt more quickly to family life in their new homes. However, this does not mean that kennel-reared puppies cannot adapt equally well to family life if their basic temperaments are good and as long as the breeder makes the effort to socialise and play with the pups regularly.

Making The Choice

When it comes to choosing your puppy, you may find that an experienced breeder will guide you towards a puppy whose personality will, hopefully, suit your family best. This can be very helpful, as it is often a difficult decision to pick just one from several, equally delightful, puppies. If you are invited to make your own choice, it is often tempting to pick the boldest puppy, the one that comes to you first, pushing his littermates aside. However, the boldest puppy with the pushy personality can be quite challenging if you are an inexperienced owner. In this situation, you would be better off choosing a more middle-of-the-road pup – one that is not too bold but not shy either.

This puppy is bred from working lines.

A puppy bred from show lines

PROSPECTIVE CAREERS

Although many people choose a Cocker purely as a family pet, some owners are looking for a Cocker for a specific purpose, such as showing or working. In such cases, the above advice is equally applicable, but there are a few extra considerations, too. If you want to get involved in showing or working your Cocker, you must be prepared to do some further research and make sure the breeders you contact have the type of dog you are looking for and also the necessary experience to guide you towards a puppy with the potential to succeed in your chosen activity.

If you want to show your Cocker, you will need to find a breeder that actively shows their own dogs and is successful. As mentioned earlier, there are many breeders of show-type dogs, but puppies bred by those who breed purely for the pet market will not necessarily be of the standard required for the show ring. Of course, it is never possible to guarantee that any promising puppy will grow up to be a successful show dog, but if you choose the right breeder, he or she should be able to advise which puppies show the most potential. Bearing this in mind, there are some things to look out for which would rule a puppy out of being a show dog: for example, patches of white anywhere other than the chest on a solid-coloured dog, or only one testicle on a male pup (although missing testicles can come down as a puppy grows).

If you are looking to work your dog, then the same advice applies: find a breeder who works his dogs successfully and has the experience to guide you in your choice of pup. As with show dogs, there can never be a guarantee that every Working Cocker pup will make a good worker, but buying from an experienced breeder will give you a head start at least.

CHOOSING A RESCUED DOG

Although many people get their first Cocker as a puppy from a breeder, it should be remembered that there are many lovely dogs in rescue, often through no fault of their own. So if you are looking for a Cocker and do not necessarily want one at eight weeks from a breeder, you may find there is rescued dog that would suit your home and lifestyle perfectly. Make sure any rescue organisation you contact is reputable, as dog rescues are not currently regulated in any way. Reputable rescues will assess a

dog as much as possible before rehoming and will also check out any potential new owners to make sure they can offer the right home for each particular dog. A good rescue will also offer back-up advice and support after a dog goes to a new home and will always take back a dog if this ever becomes necessary.

It can be very rewarding to give an older dog a new home.

Settling In

ntroducing a new Cocker puppy into the family is exciting but it can also be quite daunting if you are new to puppy ownership. The information below will help you prepare for your new arrival and ensure the initial settling-in period goes as smoothly as possible.

IN THE GARDEN

It is important for your puppy to have access to a safe, secure space outside to make house-training easier and to give him room to play. Before you bring your pup home, check that your garden is totally secure. Puppies can squeeze through the smallest gaps, so make sure your fencing is in good repair and is high enough for an adult Cocker (as a guide, a 5ft/1.5m fence will offer the necessary security).

A Cocker puppy is an enthusiastic gardener so you will need to protect plants and shrubs that you value.

If you have a garden pond, either fence it off temporarily, or make sure it is covered so your puppy cannot fall in accidentally.

Cocker puppies often love to chew plants and dig holes in the garden. If you are very proud of your garden and have a number of precious shrubs or plants, it can help to protect individual plants or temporarily fence off a part of the garden just for the puppy's use. Caution is also needed if your garden contains plants or shrubs that are poisonous when eaten by dogs. There is not the room to list all such plants here, but common examples include the laburnum tree, rhododendron, daffodil and crocus bulbs. On a similar note, ensure all dangerous garden chemicals are kept securely locked away where your puppy cannot reach them.

IN THE HOME

As well as making sure your garden is safe, it is also a good idea to check that your house is as puppy-proofed as possible. This means making sure any dangling cables are safely secured and any other hazards, such as potentially poisonous houseplants or household cleaners/medicines, are well out of a puppy's reach. If your children are in the habit of leaving their toys lying around, teach them to pick them up and store them in a toy box, particularly if they play with small plastic models, which could be easily swallowed by a puppy.

You might also want to invest in a safety gate to stop your puppy from going upstairs; young puppies should not be encouraged to run up and down stairs or steep steps, as it can be damaging for their immature growth plates. Safety gates are also useful if your house has an open-plan layout, as you can use one to block off your puppy's access to any room containing expensive carpets or furniture, at least until he is house-trained and past the chewing phase.

BUYING EQUIPMENT

There is a vast array of different products on the market aimed at new puppy owners. Not all are essential, but here are the most important items your puppy will need:

Bed

Many new owners will buy a crate (see below), which will be used as their puppy's bed. However, if you prefer not to use a crate or want an additional bed, it is best to opt for the hard, plastic variety available in a variety of colours and sizes. Plastic beds are easily cleaned and can be lined with a comfy, soft blanket or a piece of the popular polyester fleece bedding. They are also more durable and less likely to be chewed than fabric beds, bean bags or the traditional wicker basket.

Dog crate/puppy pen

Crates are now very popular, and, when used correctly, they can help in house-training as well as providing your puppy with his own cosy 'den' in the house. Many owners use a crate or bed in combination with a

Your Cocker will appreciate having a bed he can use whenever he chooses.

puppy pen made of mesh panels that clip together. The crate/bed is placed inside the pen, giving the puppy a larger area where he can be securely left for reasonable periods of time. If you intend using a crate, with or without a pen, it is important to remember that it should not be used to contain your pup for long periods of time; nor should it be used as a place of punishment for "naughty" behaviour.

A crate needs to be somewhere a puppy feels safe and secure so you need to make it as attractive as possible with soft bedding, some toys and perhaps a cover over the top to make it even cosier. You should also feed your pup his meals in the crate and throw treats in there from time to time. Never shut a puppy inside a crate with the door closed until he is happy to go in there voluntarily throughout the day with the door open. This process can take some time but should never be rushed if you want crate training to be a success.

Bowls

A puppy will require one bowl for his food and one for water. There are various types of bowls available, ranging from easily washed plastic and stainless steel to heavy pottery/stoneware bowls. Heavier bowls are best for water, as they are

Start with a small bowl – you will need a bigger bowl when your puppy's ears grow longer.

not easily picked up and moved around. Your puppy will only need a small food bowl to begin with, but as he gets bigger and his ears grow longer, you could invest in a spaniel bowl. Spaniel bowls are taller than average bowls and are designed with tapered sides so that the ears drop either side of the bowl, rather than dangling in the food (as is often the case with flatter bowls).

Collar/lead

Puppy collars and leads are available in a range of colours and materials to suit all tastes. Nylon collars may be best for puppies, as these often offer more room for expansion as the puppy grows, compared to traditional leather collars. They are also washable, lightweight and are not easily chewed. Matching leads are usually available when buying this kind of collar.

The toys you buy will need to be suitably robust.

Some owners prefer the feel of a leather collar and lead (leather softens with use, unlike nylon). If you prefer to buy a leather collar when your pup is older, look for a round, sewn collar (rather than a flat collar) as these are better than flat collars for longhaired dogs. Don't forget that you will also need an identity tag attached to the collar when taking your puppy out in public. This is a legal requirement and must contain your name and address including your postcode. A telephone number is optional but highly recommended.

When buying a first lead for your puppy (whether leather or nylon), make sure it is not too long – a shorter lead is better for puppies and will give you more control when lead training.

Retractable/extending leads are popular and can be useful for allowing some freedom in areas where off-lead exercise is not possible (e.g. when walking on paths near sheep or cattle). However, they should be used with caution; they can encourage pulling on the lead and should never be used for road/pavement walking (it is too easy to forget to put the lead into the lock position, meaning a dog can pull into the road and cause an accident).

Toys
Many owners buy a multitude of expensive toys but find their puppies prefer the homemade variety! Empty plastic bottles and cardboard boxes will often keep a puppy entertained for hours, although the owner will need to carefully supervise and remove such items once they start to disintegrate. Puppies often like soft,

Finding A Vet

Finding the right veterinary practice is very important for new puppy owners. Often the best way to find a good vet is to ask for recommendations from other dog-owning family members or friends/neighbours. If this is not possible, you could use telephone directories to locate details of vets in your area, then visit the practices concerned. Check what facilities are on offer, whether the staff members seem friendly and approachable and whether the opening hours are convenient for you.

You also need to find out what kind of 24-hour cover is provided for emergencies. Some practices use their own vets to provide emergency cover; others will share cover with neighbouring practices. The advantage of in-house emergency cover is that you will, hopefully, see someone who already knows you and your dog if you need to call the vet out of hours. Finally, you should ask whether the practice is accredited by the Royal College of Veterinary Surgeons. This voluntary scheme gives accredited status to practices that have been inspected and found to meet various stringent standards of veterinary care.

furry toys too, but care must be taken to remove any easily swallowed plastic parts first. It is best to avoid giving soft toys to your puppy if you have children with similar toys, as your pup will not be able to tell the difference between the two.

Other types of toy that your pup may enjoy include rope tug toys and nylon bones (which can help when teething), balls (but not too small to avoid the risk of your puppy accidentally swallowing one) and rubber activity toys like Kongs (which can be filled with tasty treats to keep your pup occupied for

Grooming Kit

A puppy grooming kit should include a slicker brush, which is a square or rectangular brush with metal pins. It is better to buy a soft slicker to begin with, as these are kinder on a puppy's more delicate skin. You will also need two combs, one with medium-spaced teeth and one with fine teeth. A pair of straight-edged scissors (for trimming excess hair from around your puppy's feet) is also useful. Later you may want to invest in other tools and equipment (see the section on Grooming in Chapter 4), but you will only need the basic brush and combs to start with.

longer). To keep your puppy interested in his toys, try to rotate them so he does not have access to all his toys all the time. Keep some toys back as 'special' and use them only for training sessions or when leaving your pup alone for a while. These 'special' toys will still have the novelty factor if your pup does not see them all the time and so will be more attractive to him.

ARRIVING HOME

It is better to collect your puppy from the breeder as early in the day as possible, especially if you are travelling some distance. This means your puppy will have plenty of time to adjust to his new home and get to know his new family before it is time for bed. This should make it easier for him to settle on his first night.

MEETING THE FAMILY

It is a big step for any puppy to leave the security of his breeder and his existing canine family, so be prepared for it to take some time for your puppy to settle into his new home. Try not to overwhelm him with too much noise and excitement to begin with.

If you have children, they will be very excited at welcoming a new puppy and will want to pick him up and hold him. But puppies often do not enjoy being picked up, and it can also be dangerous if a child walks around while holding a puppy; puppies squirm and wriggle and could easily fall to the ground, resulting in injury. Encourage your children only to hold the puppy when they are sitting down. Also teach them that puppies get tired very easily so they should never disturb a pup if he is sleeping.

You may have other family members and friends who are keen to come and meet your new arrival. Meeting new people is an important part in your puppy's socialisation, but try to ensure he is not overwhelmed with visitors during his settling-in period, as this could be exhausting for a pup already adjusting to so many other new experiences.

At last it is time to collect your puppy and bring him home.

INTRODUCING HOUSE PETS

If you already have an older dog in your home, it is best to introduce your new pup on reasonably neutral territory. If the pup is too young to have been vaccinated, your garden would be the best place for introductions to take place. Ideally, put your pup in the garden and then let the resident dog out to find him, under close supervision. Once they have been introduced, both dogs can come into the house together.

Sometimes a resident dog will accept a new puppy immediately and will be keen to play with the new arrival. Care should be taken that play sessions are not allowed to become too rough, as a bigger dog could accidentally injure a young pup during

Be patient when you introduce a new puppy to a resident dog.

putting a stair gate across the stairs so that your cat/s can get upstairs but the pup cannot. You will also need to ensure that cat feeding bowls and litter trays are placed where your puppy cannot reach them.

Small pets, such as rabbits and guinea pigs, are best kept in secure pens or runs when you have a new puppy. Puppies can be taught not to chase small pets, but this will take time and it is best not to take any chances initially. If your small pets are used to spending short periods running around outside of their pens, then you can still do this, but your pup will need to be safely contained, perhaps behind a safety gate or in a dog crate.

over-boisterous play. On the other hand, a resident dog may, initially, be very suspicious of a new puppy and may take weeks to fully accept the 'incomer'. If this happens, you should be patient and ensure the older dog always has his own space where he can get some peace and quiet away from the puppy. Contact between the two should be carefully supervised during this time.

Care should also be taken when introducing a puppy to a home with other resident pets. If you have a cat or cats, they need to have an area where they can get away from the puppy if necessary. This could mean

FEEDING

A reputable breeder will supply new owners with a detailed diet sheet, giving information on food, suggested amounts and meal timings. Most will also provide a small supply of food so that the puppy can continue to eat what he is used to during the settling-in period in a new home. This helps to avoid stomach upsets and offers the pup some continuity at a time when everything else is changing.

If you wish to change your puppy's food, it is best to wait a week at least and then gradually start mixing the new food with the old food over a period of a few days. A sudden change of diet can result in stomach upsets.

Puppies leaving for their new homes at eight weeks old will usually be on four meals a day. At this age, their stomachs are small and so they need small meals spaced out over the day. Generally, it is best to leave around four hours between meals to give time for each meal to be digested. As puppies grow, their stomachs can take bigger meals and it becomes possible to reduce the frequency of meal times. From four months old, most puppies will be on three meals a day and this then goes down to two meals at six months old and onwards.

You might find that your puppy goes off his food when he first arrives home. Some puppies lose their appetites temporarily due to the excitement of a new home. This soon passes as long as you do not panic and immediately start offering your pup different types of food to tempt him to eat. All this does is teach him that if he does not eat what is offered, he will be given something different next time. To avoid creating

Do not be alarmed if your puppy is reluctant to eat to begin with.

a fussy puppy, you should put his food down at the appropriate time, and, if it is not eaten after 15 minutes or so, the bowl should be removed and nothing else offered until it is time for the next meal. You may have to repeat this process for a few days, but eventually your pup should settle into a normal eating routine, realising that if he does not eat what is in his bowl, he goes without.

HOUSE TRAINING

House training a new puppy can be a long process and not something that can be accomplished in a few days. Young puppies have little bladder control to start off with and short attention spans. They do not always remember where they are supposed

The key to successful house training is establishing a routine so your puppy understands what is required.

to toilet and are not capable of controlling their bladders or bowels for long periods. Indeed, it can take months before a puppy is reliably house-trained so you need to be prepared for this.

Here are a few key things to remember:

- Do not expect your puppy to train himself by leaving the door open or just letting him outside while you stay inside. You must go outside with your puppy (whatever the weather) and wait with him until he does the necessary. Use a key phrase every time you want your puppy to go to the toilet. This phrase, such as "Hurry up" or "Be quick", will eventually become associated in your pup's mind with toileting outside and you will be able to use it to command your puppy to 'go' wherever you are – at home or on a walk.

- Praise your puppy quietly for toileting in the right place. It is important to reward good behaviour, so use your voice to praise or offer a small treat, but do not go overboard or your pup will get over excited.

- Take your puppy outside frequently, at least every one to two hours initially. He will need to go whenever he wakes up from a sleep, after he has eaten, and after he has had an active play session. Excitement or stress can also make a puppy want to go to the toilet, so be aware of this. It can feel at this stage that you are always taking your puppy outside, but this hard work will pay off in the long run, providing you are consistent.

- Never punish your puppy if you discover an accident in the home. It is in order to calmly but firmly say "No, outside" if you catch your

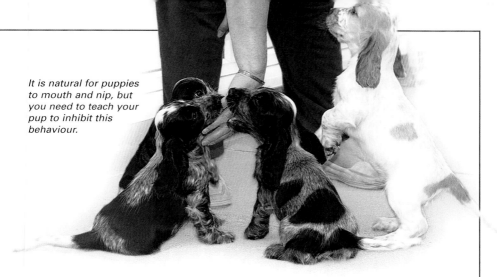

It is natural for puppies to mouth and nip, but you need to teach your pup to inhibit this behaviour.

pup doing a puddle inside. But it is pointless and cruel to punish a puppy for something that he did even minutes ago, as he will have no idea why you are cross. Clean up any accidents calmly and without fuss. Remember to use either biological washing detergent or specialist urine cleaner rather than normal household disinfectants, as these may contain ammonia, which can attract puppies back to the same spot.

- Some owners like to use newspaper or puppy training pads inside as an aid to house-training. However, this approach can make the whole process take longer as, inadvertently, the owner is teaching the puppy that it is acceptable to toilet in some areas inside the home. This can be confusing, as the puppy is getting mixed messages about where he

can toilet. It is far better to concentrate totally on teaching a puppy to only 'go' outside by taking him out at every available opportunity.

PLAY BITING

All puppies mouth and play bite; it is how they explore the world around them and also how they play with their littermates in the nest. Many new owners are alarmed by this behaviour and worry that they have an aggressive, untypical puppy. In fact, play biting is completely normal and very important to a puppy's development, as it helps him to learn bite inhibition (i.e. not to bite too hard). Having said that, puppies do have to learn not to bite their human family members, but this process takes time and patience and a consistent approach from all the family.

There are several techniques that can be effective when teaching a puppy not to bite; some will be more effective than others, depending on the individual puppy:

- Yelp loudly (as if in pain) whenever your puppy bites. This can be enough to interrupt the behaviour so that you can then distract your puppy by offering one of his own chew toys. However, for some puppies, yelping will just increase their excitement, causing them to bite even more.
- Time-outs involve withdrawing your attention from your puppy for a short time, either by removing yourself from the room or by removing your puppy and placing him in another room by himself. Time-outs need to be kept short – just a few minutes – as puppies do not understand long periods of being ignored.
- Stay calm. All family members need to stay calm, as shouting at a puppy will just increase his adrenalin levels, making him bite more. Children should be taught to sit or stand still "like a statue", making no eye contact with the pup, rather than jumping or running about when the puppy bites their toes! An over-excited pup will soon calm down if nobody is reacting to his behaviour.

THE FIRST NIGHT

Puppies need time to adjust to sleeping without the company of their littermates in a totally new environment. Breeders often supply an old piece of bedding and perhaps a soft toy, which smell familiar to the pup. If you place these in your pup's bed or crate, they can be very comforting and help your pup to sleep in his new home.

The old-fashioned

To begin with your puppy will miss the company of his littermates.

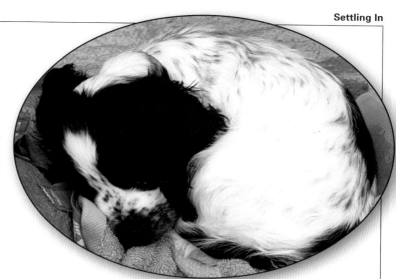

You may decide to allow your puppy to sleep in your bedroom for the first couple of nights.

approach to a puppy's first night – and one still popular with some owners – is to decide where the puppy will sleep, usually in a kitchen or utility room, and then put him to bed and ignore cries or howls of distress for however long it takes for the pup to fall asleep. This approach will work eventually, but it is arguably unnecessarily harsh and could also lead to neighbour problems if you live in a modern house with thin walls. A puppy that is left to howl will also invariably make a mess overnight, as distress increases the urge to go to the toilet.

A more sympathetic approach is to gradually introduce the puppy to the idea of sleeping alone by either having the puppy in your bedroom for a while or by sleeping close to the puppy downstairs for a few days. This approach is often very successful and does not result in a spoiled puppy unable to sleep alone. It just makes the settling-in stage easier and less stressful for everyone. Having your puppy's crate or bed near you at night also helps in the house-training process, as you will hear him whimper if he needs to go outside and you can then take him out quickly before any accidents occur.

A compromise between the above two methods is to decide where your puppy will sleep as before, but commit to getting up once or twice in the night so that pup can go outside to relieve himself. If you are doing this, avoid making a big fuss of your pup, as this will encourage him to be clingy and demand your company. Calmly and quickly take your pup outside and then put him straight back to bed afterwards without fussing him or playing with him. If your puppy continues to cry, even after being outside, try not to go back down to him unless this is unavoidable. If you go to him every time he cries, he will quickly learn that this is a guaranteed way of getting your attention.

A RESCUED DOG

If you are introducing a rescued Cocker (or older dog from a breeder) into your family rather than a new puppy, there are a few guidelines that will help your new family member adjust to his new home.

The most important thing is not to make too much of a fuss of your rescue dog in an attempt to compensate for any previous bad experiences or because you feel sorry for a dog that has had to find a new home. Too much attention can make a rescued dog clingy and lead to separation anxiety problems. It is far better to treat your new dog as if he has always been a member of your family by starting as you mean to go on, keeping to a normal routine as far as possible.

Get your new dog used to being left alone for short periods from the start so that he does not become over-dependent on your company. Providing activity toys, such as a Kong stuffed with tasty treats, will keep your dog occupied while you are out.

Rescued dogs need time and space to settle into a new home. This can take weeks or even months, depending on the dog's previous background and

An older dog needs time and space to settle and feel confident in a new home.

experiences. You need to make allowances for this and not expect too much, too soon. You should also be prepared to undertake house-training, as even previously house-trained rescued dogs can lapse when in a new home for the first time. Some rescues may also have come from kennels and have never been house-trained. In these cases, treat your dog like a puppy and go back to basics, using the house-training tips provided earlier.

If you already have a dog and are introducing a rescued Cocker to your home, much of the same advice on introducing a puppy to an existing dog applies, particularly the need to introduce the two dogs on neutral territory where possible. Once introduced, let the two dogs sort out their own relationship without interference unless unavoidable. Sometimes owners favour the resident dog in an attempt to ensure he remains top dog in the new canine hierarchy, but this is something the two dogs need to work out for themselves if there is to be a harmonious household. Trying to enforce a particular hierarchy between two or more dogs can cause problems and should be avoided.

It is advisable to allow two adult dogs to sort out their own relationship.

Caring For A Cocker

When a Cocker Spaniel comes into your home, you are responsible for all his needs, providing the correct diet and exercise to suit his age and lifestyle, and ensuring that he has the routine care that will keep him fit and healthy.

CHOOSING A DIET

A healthy Cocker needs a balanced diet that contains the right amounts of proteins, fats, carbohydrates, fibre, vitamins and minerals. However, there is no single diet available that is guaranteed to suit every Cocker for the whole of his life. Just like humans, dogs are all individuals and what suits one dog may not suit another. A dog's dietary needs may change according to his age and his lifestyle – for example, a growing, active puppy needs a very different diet to an elderly, less active dog. The important thing is to find the right diet that suits your Cocker at each relevant stage of his life

You need to find a diet that meets the needs of your Cocker.

Commercial dog diets

Complete dry foods have become very popular for reasons of cost and convenience. Owners like the fact they can just pour the appropriate amount of kibble in their dog's bowl with minimum fuss and effort. Many Cockers enjoy complete dry dog foods and thrive on this type of diet. However, it has to be said that not all dry dog foods are equal. There can be a considerable difference in the quality of ingredients of a cheaper brand compared to a more expensive, premium brand.

Cheaper brands often contain more cereal content than real meat; cereals (such as wheat, maize, corn) provide a form of protein that is inexpensive, but is less easily digested than good-quality proteins like red meat and chicken. Some dogs also develop intolerances to foods with a high cereal content, resulting in digestive upsets or skin irritation. Cheaper complete foods usually contain artificial colours and preservatives, which may make the food more attractive to human eyes but have been linked with possible hyperactivity in some dogs.

If you have decided you would like

to feed your Cocker on a complete dry dog food, remember that you get what you pay for. A good-quality complete food may appear more expensive initially, but you will usually have to feed less than you would a cheaper brand because the food has better, more easily digestible ingredients. Check the ingredients listed on the bag and look for a food with a high content of real meat, with a named protein source (chicken, lamb, fish etc) as the first ingredient, and as few additives as possible. These are signs of a good-quality food that uses the best ingredients to keep your Cocker health and happy.

Some owners prefer to feed a 'wet' food, supplied in sealed pouches or cans, as these are often more palatable to dogs, particularly if you have a fussy eater. However, it again pays to check the ingredients list, as some cans or pouches contain artificial colours and additives and have a high sugar content. Better-quality wet foods contain only high-quality ingredients, such as meat, vegetables and rice, but this invariably adds to the cost of what is already a relatively expensive way of feeding your dog, in comparison to dry complete foods.

NATURAL DIETS

At one time, the traditional way of feeding a dog was to mix raw or cooked meat with a biscuit meal or perhaps with rice. Vegetable scraps from the family table would often also be added. Many dogs lived long, happy lives on this kind of diet and there is no reason why owners today cannot continue to feed a home-prepared diet along these lines.

Dogs find canned or 'wet' food very appetising, but you must ensure it is of a suitable quality to provide a nutritious diet.

Check the ingredients carefully before choosing a complete diet.

There is certainly an argument that the use of freshly prepared, more natural ingredients is better for the health of dogs, just as it is for humans. However, care must be taken to ensure a home-prepared diet offers the right balance of vitamins and minerals. If you are worried about this, a vitamin supplement can be added to the food, but you should never exceed the recommended dose, as some vitamins can be harmful to dogs when given in excess.

The BARF (bones and raw food, or biologically appropriate raw food) diet goes further than the home-prepared traditional diet and involves feeding purely raw food and bones, replicating the diet of a wild dog as far as possible. It is argued that a completely raw, natural diet results in many benefits, e.g. fewer anal gland problems, better skin and coat condition, improved digestion and cleaner teeth. Although this diet is considered controversial by many in the veterinary profession, it is gaining in popularity with owners. If this is something that interests you, then do your research first and buy at least one book on the subject so you have a good basic grounding on what you will need to raise your Cocker on this diet.

FEEDING REGIME

How often you feed your Cocker will depend on his age. Growing puppies need regular small meals spaced out throughout the day, starting with four meals from eight weeks old and eventually going down to two meals a day from six months old. Traditionally, many dogs were only fed once a day when they reached adulthood, from 12 months onwards, but owners often find that their adult Cockers are happier continuing on a regime of two meals a day, usually fed morning and late afternoon or evening.

It is better to provide set meal times for your dog, as free feeding, where a bowl of food is left down all day long and is continually topped up,

An eight-week-old puppy will need four meals a day.

You need to take into account your Cocker's age and lifestyle when planning a diet.

can encourage over-eating and make it very difficult to monitor how much a dog is actually eating, particularly in a home with more than one dog. Fixed meal times also makes it easier to predict when your dog needs to go outside to toilet; bowel movements often follow a meal, especially in young puppies.

How much to feed

How much to feed your Cocker will depend on various factors, such as his age, whether he is neutered, and how active he is. Growing puppies need relatively more food than they will as adults to ensure optimum development. Neutered Cockers can be prone to weight gain so may need less food than before and, perhaps, a change in diet to one of the specially formulated low-calorie dog foods. The same applies to older Cockers, who become less active as they age and so need less food; they also need a lower level of protein than is found in foods aimed at young dogs. On the other hand, very active dogs, such as working dogs or those who take part in activities like agility, may need an increase in the amount fed and perhaps a diet with higher levels of fat and protein to maintain their energy levels and optimum weight.

If you are feeding a commercial dog food, the manufacturer will supply information on suggested feeding amounts per age of

Bones And Chews

Most dogs love to use their jaws and teeth to chew; chewing is relaxing for your dog and also helps to maintain good dental health. Teething puppies will often chew constantly, as it helps to relieve the pain of the new teeth coming through.

There is a huge variety of commercially prepared bones and chews on the market, ranging from beef hide chews to hard, plastic bones. If you are buying rawhide chews for your Cocker, it is best to go for the larger, pressed type, as these will not be so easily swallowed and destroyed. Raw marrow bones are also enjoyed by many dogs but are perhaps best not given to young puppies, as they can be too rich for their stomachs. Never feed cooked bones to your dog, as cooking makes bones brittle and prone to splintering, which can be very dangerous.

While most chews and bones of the appropriate size are considered safe, none is totally without risk, so you should always supervise your dog while he is enjoying his chew. If you find that your Cocker is able to chew large pieces off his bone or chew, remove it immediately, as these pieces could be swallowed and result in an intestinal blockage.

puppy/dog, but this should be treated as a rough guide only. You may need to adjust these amounts based on what your own hands and eyes tell you about whether your Cocker is carrying the right amount of weight or not. You also need to take into account any treats you give during training sessions, as these need to be included in your Cocker's daily allowance, particularly if he is prone to weight gain.

Kennel Dogs

While it is not unusual for groups of working and show Cockers to be kept outside in suitable kennels, particularly in rural areas, a single pet Cocker will not generally settle outside and will prefer to be with his family inside the family home. There are problems associated with kennelling, such as the increased risk of theft – many pedigree dogs have been stolen from apparently secure kennels and gardens. In addition, kennel dogs can be noisy, since they may howl out of boredom or alarm bark at outside distractions, such as neighbourhood cats entering the garden or people walking along the street. This can result in complaints from neighbours, especially in urban areas.

Assessing your Cocker's weight

If your Cocker is carrying the right amount of weight – not too fat and not too thin – you should be able to feel your dog's ribs but not see them, and he should have a noticeable waist with his body narrowing slightly after the ribs. If you cannot easily feel the ribs, then it may be time to reduce the amount fed. On the other hand, if the ribs are too prominent and your dog feels overly bony along the spine, you may need to increase his food.

Sometimes Cocker puppies and adults grow heavy coats, which give the illusion of a fat dog when this is not the case. Feeling underneath the thick hair or puppy fluff with your hands should tell you whether your Cocker is indeed overweight or not.

HOLIDAYS

Holidaying with your Cocker can be fun! There are now many holiday properties where pets are welcome, but understandably the popular ones are booked well in advance, so it is best not to leave arrangements until the last minute.

If you are able to take your Cocker on holiday, he will relish the change of scene.

It is also possible to travel with your Cocker outside of the UK, but this does mean meeting the requirements of the Pet Passport Scheme to the letter (in relation to vaccinations, blood tests, tick and flea treatments etc.). Holidaying abroad with your dog does, however, bring increased risks, as there are a number of diseases found in other countries that do not exist here as yet. If you are travelling to warmer countries, it should be considered that your Cocker may not enjoy the hotter temperatures even if you do.

If you decide to go on holiday without your Cocker, you will need to make suitable arrangements for his care well in advance. Boarding kennels are popular with many owners, but these can vary in quality, so it is a good idea to ask for personal recommendations from your dog-owning friends. Visit kennels first and make sure you are happy with the conditions and services offered. If you do not want to use boarding kennels, there are various agencies offering pet-sitting services in the home. Again, ask for personal recommendations where possible and check that any company used is fully licensed and insured.

Accustom your puppy to being groomed from an early age.

GROOMING

The Cocker is a longhaired breed and so needs regular grooming to keep the coat knot-free and in good condition. Show-type Cockers have thicker, longer coats than working type dogs, but all Cockers will need to learn to accept being groomed on a regular basis. Start your grooming routine as soon as your puppy comes home so that he gets used to the idea long before his coat is thick enough to require extensive grooming.

Always groom your Cocker on a raised surface or table otherwise you may find that you have to chase him around the floor on your hands and knees, which is not conducive to a successful grooming session! Make sure the surface of your table is non-slip by placing either a rubber mat or small piece of carpet on the top. This is not necessary if you invest in a purpose-made grooming table.

As mentioned in Chapter Three, your basic grooming kit should include a slicker brush, combs and straight-edged scissors. You may eventually also want to buy items such as thinning scissors, nail clippers, coat stripping tools and, perhaps, electric clippers.

Regular daily routine

Spend a few minutes every day gently brushing your puppy all over with a slicker brush. Reward your puppy for standing still, even if it is just for a few seconds at first. Eventually, he will stand for longer periods, but it will take patience and lots of practice before this is achieved, so you will need to persevere.

Teach your puppy to lie on his back

while you brush under his elbows and in the groin area, where knots often appear as the coat grows. Comb through his ears and also check his nails to see if they need clipping. You can use ordinary 'human' nail clippers for puppy nails, but you will need to invest in dog nail clippers for adult nails.

As your puppy grows, his coat will usually grow thicker and longer, particularly if he comes from show lines. This means he will need a more thorough grooming session – perhaps 10 to 15 minutes a day. You should comb through the ear and body feathering, using your medium-toothed comb, to ensure there are no knots left anywhere. You can also use your slicker brush to remove any loose hair from the top coat or to brush out small tangles from the feathering.

Puppy feet can become quite hairy, so you should use your small scissors to trim excess hair from under and around the foot. You could also check inside the ears and use your scissors to snip away excess hair.

Eventually, many show-type Cocker puppies will reach a stage where more extensive trimming is needed over and above regular daily grooming. When this time comes, usually at five to six months of age onwards, you will need to decide which type of trim is most suitable for you and your Cocker.

Show trim

Show Cockers are trimmed using the traditional method of hand stripping where excess dead hair is plucked out, using finger and thumb, or stripped out with a small, fine-toothed comb, often known as a spaniel comb. This is a long process,

SHOW PRESENTATION: HAND STRIPPING

The traditional method of hand stripping is used to remove dead hair.

The whole body has to be stripped, working along the body to the hindquarters.

SHOW PRESENTATION: TRIMMING

Thinning scissors are used to remove excess hair so the coat lies flat.

The hair behind the ears needs to be thinned out.

The coat on the hindquarters, known as the 'trousers', also needs attention.

Straight scissors are used to tidy up the feathering.

The paws are trimmed to show off the correct shape.

The long coat on the undercarriage is trimmed.

The finished result: A show dog looks glamorous, but should still retain a natural appearance.

requiring a considerable degree of skill, but it produces a lovely, natural finish, which lasts longer than other methods. Patience is needed, as coats can only be stripped out when the hair is ready to come out naturally, which can be as late as nine months or even older in some dogs.

Clippers and other tools with blades should never be used on show Cockers, as they cut the coat and result in an unnatural finish. Feathering under the body and on the legs and ears is left long but will be shaped and thinned out where necessary with thinning scissors. Straight-edged scissors are used to keep the feet tidy.

If you want to show your Cocker or you would like your pet Cocker to be trimmed in the traditional way, you may need to learn how to hand strip your dog yourself, as very few professional groomers are able to provide this service due to the time it takes. However, some Cocker breeders and exhibitors do provide a hand stripping service or are willing to offer tuition to a keen newcomer. Failing that, there are grooming videos and booklets available, which offer advice and demonstrate the necessary techniques.

Pet trim

A sympathetic pet trim for both Cocker types involves removing excess body hair with either a combination of thinning scissors and stripping tools, or with electric clippers. Clippers do a quick, efficient job, but the effect is less natural than the scissors/stripping tool approach. Feathering is thinned out and trimmed much shorter than for a show dog.

Some groomers will clip all the feathering off, which undoubtedly

PET GROOMING: CLIPPING

If you decide to keep your Cocker in pet trim, you can use electric clippers so that the coat is easy to manage.

PET GROOMING: TRIMMING

Feathering will need to be trimmed, and you will also need to keep a check on the underside.

The finished result: With less feathering, a pet trim is easy to maintain.

makes for easy maintenance between trims but can look rather unattractive. Sometimes, if the coat is badly matted, there is no choice but to do this. However, it will look more natural if a pet Cocker is left with a little feathering on the legs and underneath the body.

If you opt for a pet trim for your Cocker, you can buy the necessary tools and learn to do this yourself, which saves money in the long run, or you can pay for a professional groomer's services. You will need to visit a professional groomer every eight to 12 weeks approximately and, as with other canine services, it pays to do your homework and find one by personal recommendation if possible.

Neutering And Cocker Coats

Neutering results in hormonal changes that can affect the coats of many Cockers, including working-strain dogs. These changes can take months to be noticeable, but owners will often find that coats become thicker and coarser, and, eventually, hand stripping ceases to be an option, as the coat no longer comes out naturally. When this happens, the usual solution is to use electric clippers to keep the coat neat and tidy.

Bathing

There is no hard-and-fast rule about how often you should bath your Cocker. As a general guide, bath your dog when you feel he needs it, particularly if he has got very muddy or has rolled in something particularly unpleasant, as Cockers often do. Do not be afraid to bath your puppy. Getting a young puppy used to the sensation of being bathed and the noise of the hairdryer means these experiences will hold no fear for him as he grows up.

Place a rubber non-slip mat in the bath or basin to stop your dog's feet from sliding about and always use a dog/puppy shampoo formulated to suit a dog's skin and coat. When bathing an adult Cocker with a thicker coat, follow up the shampoo with a good conditioner, as this will make the feathering easy to groom and less prone to tangles.

Regular checks

During your regular daily grooming sessions, you should practise opening and examining your puppy's mouth, inspecting his ears, and touching his feet and nails, including any dew claws situated inside the leg above the foot. This will be very useful in the future, as your Cocker

REGULAR CHECKS

Teeth will need brushing if there is an accumulation of tartar.

Dirt can collect in the ear canals so regular cleaning is required.

Wipe debris from the eyes with a piece of damp cotton-wool.

Nails will need trimming on a routine basis.

will be used to being handled and will accept veterinary examinations when necessary without any fuss. It also means you will be immediately alerted to any problems that might need attention – for example, discharge from the ear, indicating an ear infection.

Grooming and checking the ear feathering regularly will also help you to spot any grass seeds picked up in your dog's feathering in the summer months. These seeds can cause intense pain and irritation if they find their way into the ear canal.

EXERCISE

The amount of exercise your Cocker will need depends largely on how old he is and also whether he is a show-type or a working-type dog.

Young puppies should not be over-exercised, as this can put too much strain on immature joints and growth plates, resulting in arthritis in later life and possibly contributing to the development of hip dysplasia in genetically susceptible dogs.

For puppies, a good general guide is to allow five minutes of formal exercise per month of age until fully grown. For a four-month-old puppy, this would mean that walks should last for about 20 minutes. Two short walks a day combined with normal play sessions in the garden are normally more than sufficient for a puppy of this age. As your pup gets older, you can gradually increase the length of his walks, still following the five-minute rule until he is fully grown at around 10 months of age.

Adult Cockers can usually take as much exercise as their owner is willing to provide, although, of course, there should be a gradual build-up to any really long-distance hikes. Many show-type Cockers will happily accept two moderate walks a day (30-40 minutes each approximately) with perhaps longer walks at weekends and during the holidays. These walks should include some opportunity for off-lead exercise, as there is nothing a Cocker likes more than to use his nose to investigate all the interesting scents in fields and parks.

Working Cockers may need considerably more daily exercise; if this is not provided, they can become bored and frustrated.

Young puppies will get as much exercise as they need playing in the garden.

FUN & GAMES

Exercise does not just mean walking your Cocker on the lead or letting him run about in a field. You can also play interactive games with your dog, which will exercise his body and provide mental stimulation too. Mental stimulation is very important for a busy, intelligent breed like a Cocker and will help relieve boredom and make for a calm, relaxed dog.

As a gundog breed, many Cockers naturally like to pick up items and bring them to you. You can harness this instinct by throwing balls or Frisbees and teaching your dog to retrieve them. You can also play hide and seek in the garden or in the house on a wet day. Hide dog treats or scatter a portion of your dog's daily food (if feeding a kibble) around the garden; your Cocker will happily entertain himself, rooting out the hidden treasure!

Give your Cocker the opportunity to use his nose by hiding treats in the garden.

A working Cocker will need more exercise than a Cocker from show lines.

Although this is something of a generalisation, as all Cockers are individuals, it needs to be considered if you have a dog from working lines.

Clean up!

Irresponsible dog owners who do not pick up their dogs' mess are the cause of much anti-dog feeling. When exercising your Cocker, always carry a supply of poop bags and remember to pick up after your dog every time. Dispose of used bags responsibly by placing them in either the provided dog bin or a normal public litter bin.

THE OLDER COCKER

Cockers can remain healthy and active well into their senior years although some adjustments to diet may be necessary as time goes on.

A light or senior food may be more suitable for an older Cocker if he is not as active as he was once was and particularly if he is neutered when weight gain may be an issue. Supplements such as fish oil can also be useful for the older Cocker who is becoming a little arthritic in his movement. The older Cocker will also usually appreciate a waterproof coat on wet walks and a soft, supportive bed in a draft-free area of the house.

It is a good idea to regularly check your dog's skin and coat as he ages, as older Cockers can be prone to lumps and bumps on their bodies. These are usually non-malignant fatty lumps (lipomas) and can often be safely left alone. However, all lumps should be checked out by a vet as a precaution.

Hypothyroidism is also quite

common in older Cockers. This is a hormonal condition with a range of symptoms, including hair loss, poor skin and lethargy. If your Cocker has any of these symptoms, consult your vet, who can test your dog's thyroid function and recommend the appropriate treatment where necessary.

Older Cockers should continue to be exercised for as long as they enjoy it, although they may be happier with shorter walks than before. A very elderly Cocker may no longer want to go out for formal walks but will be content with regular potters around the garden. Older dogs also need to keep their brains active, so it is important to continue to play games and offer toys as before. There are even specially designed toys for senior dogs, generally made of softer material for dogs not able to chew as hard as in their youth.

Be aware of the changing needs of your Cocker as he ages.

LETTING GO

Inevitably there will come a time when you realise that your Cocker is no longer enjoying life as he once did, either because of serious illness or simply due to the frailty of old age. Knowing when is the right time to let go of a beloved pet is one of the most difficult decisions any owner will ever have to make. Some owners find the decision so hard that they leave it too long, and, as a result, their dog suffers unnecessarily, although this is not the owner's intention. Remember that your Cocker has given you years of companionship and unconditional affection, and, in return, he deserves to be given a dignified, peaceful ending – no matter how difficult this might be for you.

The signs that the time has come to make that decision are when the bad days far outweigh the good, when you can see your Cocker has little interest in life anymore, or when he is in pain more often than he is not. You may find he no longer wants his food and prefers to stay in his bed all day, reluctant to move. Even a very ill Cocker will still try to wag his tail and lift his head to greet his family, but when this is an obvious effort, listen to what he is telling you and have the strength to make that final telephone call to your vet. Many vets will come to your home

Eventually, you will be able to look back on all the happy times you spent with your Cocker

so that your dog's last moments are as peaceful and stress-free as possible, which is particularly important if you have a Cocker who is anxious about visiting the surgery.

Saying goodbye to your Cocker will be very upsetting for all members of the family, but, in time, you will have the comfort of knowing you did the kindest thing possible and will be able to look back on all those happy times you spent together.

Educating Your Cocker

Your Cocker Spaniel puppy has a lot to learn as he grows up, and it is your job to train him to be a well-behaved canine citizen who will cope calmly in all situations. Socialisation is the process of getting your puppy used to all the different sights, sounds and experiences he is likely to come across when living in our busy, modern world. The aim is to be able to take your Cocker anywhere and in any situation and for him to remain relaxed and confident at all times.

Introduce your Cocker to a variety of different situations where he can meet people of all ages.

SOCIALISATION

The period between three and 12 weeks is a critical time in a puppy's social development. A puppy which is kept isolated during this time may become timid and never develop the confident, happy personality expected of a family pet. Good breeders will start off the socialisation process by regularly handling the pups and making sure they encounter a variety of different household noises before they leave for their new homes. However, it will be the new owner's job to continue this process before the first critical period comes to an end at 12 weeks, since most puppies will leave the breeder at around eight weeks old.

The consequences of inadequate socialisation are serious and can result in a fearful, anxious dog. Fearful dogs can often feel forced to show aggression as a way of defending themselves from whatever scares them, whether this is unfamiliar people or other dogs. Socialisation therefore plays a vital part in the development of your Cocker's social skills.

Inside And Outside The Home

As part of your programme to introduce your pup to a wide range of different people, you should encourage visitors to your home, including children of different ages, which is especially important if you do not have children yourself. Introductions should be kept as relaxed as possible, so do not allow your visitors to speak or pet your puppy until he is reacting calmly and always carefully supervise encounters with children. Young children can unintentionally hurt a puppy with rough handling.

It is also a good idea to introduce your puppy to regular callers, such as the postman/woman or milkman, so that he is happy to accept these visits to 'his' territory when he is older. Socialisation with household noises should also continue so that your pup gets used to the sounds of the vacuum cleaner, the washing machine, the television and the music player.

It is also useful to take your pup outside the home and into neighbouring streets so that he can get used to the noise of traffic. Start with a fairly quiet street and then gradually introduce busier roads as your pup becomes more confident. If you live in the countryside, you

Meeting people

You will need to introduce your puppy to as many different people as possible, including children of varying ages. Try to include people of different races, people wearing uniforms and hats, people in wheelchairs, and people pushing baby buggies. If you make a conscious effort to make your puppy's experiences with people as varied as possible, it will pay off when he is older. It can help to sit quietly with your puppy in public places where people congregate, such as outside may have to make more of an effort to find busy roads, but again such experience will pay off in the long run, as you will have a puppy unafraid of fast-moving traffic or noisy lorries. Early encounters with objects often seen in the street – such as dustbins and road bollards – are also helpful.

Later, as your puppy gains in confidence, you can take him to other locations to experience noisier environments, such as a railway or bus station. If you live in a town, you could also visit the countryside so your pup has the chance to see livestock, such as sheep, cattle and horses, being careful to observe the Countryside Code, of course.

Your Cocker needs to learn to accept that visitors to his 'territory' are not posing a threat.

supermarkets, in parks or perhaps even a car-boot sale or country fair, once you are confident your puppy can cope with this kind of experience.

Although your puppy will not be able to walk in public places until he has completed his vaccination course, this does not mean you cannot begin his socialisation process. There are puppy carriers/slings that mean you can carry your puppy about, allowing him to safely see and meet people without coming into contact with potentially unvaccinated dogs.

Allow your Cocker to meet other dogs in a calm, controlled environment.

A well socialised Cocker will take all situations in his stride.

Other dogs

Socialisation with other dogs is essential so that your puppy grows up with good doggy manners, and is able to read other dogs' body language and communicate with them without fear or aggression.

Until your puppy has completed his vaccinations, his contact with other dogs will necessarily be limited. Some vets run puppy socialisation parties for their clients. These parties can be useful if numbers are limited and if they are run by experienced staff with knowledge of puppy behaviour. However, they can turn into chaotic free-for-alls with too many puppies,

On-going Socialisation

Although the critical period for socialisation is three to 12 weeks, socialisation is not something that is over and done with once a puppy reaches a certain age. It is an ongoing process that needs to be continued and reinforced until the puppy reaches adulthood and sometimes beyond then.

Many young Cockers go through a secondary fear period, which often coincides with adolescence and the changing hormone levels at this time (six to eight months onwards). You may notice that your dog suddenly starts to shy away from things or people he was previously quite comfortable with. If this happens, you will need to go back to basics and use the same approach as you did for coping with negative experiences, remaining calm and positive and never forcing your dog to approach whatever is frightening him. With patience and careful training, this phase will soon pass.

all running about and being allowed to do what they want, including intimidating less confident pups. This type of experience could seriously affect a timid pup. An alternative would be to look for a puppy training/socialisation class run by an experienced trainer who limits the class numbers so each puppy receives individual attention at the same time as being socialised with other dogs in a calm, organised manner.

Puppies can learn a lot from sensible, older dogs who will teach the importance of good manners, tolerating a certain amount of rough play from youngsters but also

Negative Experiences

It is quite possible that at some point your puppy will become frightened by something or somebody. As negative experiences can have a long-lasting effect on puppies, you will need to handle the situation carefully. It is a natural human reaction to want to comfort a frightened animal, but too much reassurance can reinforce a puppy's fears. If your puppy is showing signs of fear, resist the temptation to pick him up for a cuddle. Try not to be too sympathetic, as an anxious puppy will get over their fear more quickly with an owner who remains cheerful and positive.

Do not force your puppy to confront his fears. Sometimes an owner will make a fearful pup go up to whatever is frightening him in an attempt to show the puppy that there is nothing to be scared of. This can put too much pressure on the puppy and make him even more fearful. It is better to aim for a gradual desensitisation over a period of time. This involves approaching the scary object at a distance to begin with, using a happy voice to praise your puppy if he does not react fearfully; you could also reward with a tasty treat at this stage. Once your puppy is comfortable with the object at a distance, you can gradually move a little closer, bit by bit, repeating the praise and reward for a non-fearful reaction. This can be a slow process, but eventually your patience will be rewarded and your puppy will have forgotten his fears.

making it clear when pups go too far. If you do not own an older dog yourself, perhaps you have friends or neighbours who have good-natured older dogs and would be happy for your puppy to be introduced to them under careful supervision.

TRAINING YOUR COCKER

Training your puppy is an essential part of your responsibilities as his owner. A well-trained Cocker is a pleasure to own; he fits happily into family life and understands what is expected of him at home and when out in public. An untrained dog is often stressed and confused, having no understanding of how to behave. He can also be a danger to himself and to others since he is not under the control of his owner.

Training is also about teamwork and developing a deeper bond with your dog. It will help you to develop a close relationship with your Cocker, resulting in a well-mannered dog whose attention is focussed on you – most of the time! Untrained dogs often have little interest in their owners and are easily distracted by outside influences, making it difficult to attract their attention or direct their behaviour in a positive way.

Training is also good exercise for the body and mind. Training sessions

The aim is to build a partnership with your Cocker so that he is happy and willing to co-operate with you.

will tire your puppy just as much as physical exercise, which is very useful in the early months when he can only go out for short walks.

Verbal communication

While dogs can learn to recognise individual words, it is important to remember that your Cocker will not be able to understand long, rambling sentences, nor will he automatically understand what individual words mean unless you teach him with

You may want to get involved with clicker training, which is a method of marking the behaviour you want with a 'click', and teaching the dog that a reward will follow.

patient repetition. He will respond more to the sound and tone of your voice than to what you actually say.

When training your dog, a calm, confident tone is needed, but you can vary the pitch according to what you are doing. For example, a high-pitched, happy tone is good for praising your dog, whereas a lower pitched, firmer tone is better for giving commands. Never lose your temper when training; shouting and yelling may make you feel better but could have a very damaging effect on your relationship with your dog, particularly if he has a sensitive nature.

Getting started

You should start training your puppy as soon as he comes home. Do not overdo it to start with – five-minute sessions are enough at first – as puppies have short attention spans and also tire quite easily. Puppy training classes are also very useful as long as the classes are not too big and the trainer uses modern, reward-based training methods, such as clicker training (such methods are more effective than the

Name Game

One of the first things you will want to do is teach your puppy his name. Start by calling his name in an excited, happy tone every time he looks up at you or starts coming towards you. Then move on to using his name to attract his attention when he is not looking at you, rewarding with a tasty treat when he responds. Keep practising this and eventually you will only need to use treats occasionally, but you should continue to offer verbal praise every time your pup responds to his name.

Your Cocker is more likely to respond to his name if he associates it only with positive experiences, so try not to use his name in a negative way when you are perhaps annoyed with him or reprimanding him.

old-fashioned punishment-based style of training). A good class will give you confidence and help you learn effective techniques that you can then put into practice at home.

One-to-one sessions with a good trainer who comes to your home can also be invaluable. You will get the benefit of your trainer's total attention and be able to ask for specific advice on any particular issue you might be struggling with, which is not always easy to do in a class situation.

TRAINING EXERCISES

Wearing a collar
It is a legal requirement for a dog to wear a collar with an identity tag when out in public, so it makes sense to get your puppy used to wearing a collar before he is officially allowed outside the home, after his vaccinations. This is usually quite easy if you start with a lightweight puppy collar and leave it on for short periods initially, and then gradually build up the time the collar is left on.

Your puppy may scratch at his neck at first, but this will soon pass once he is used to the sensation of the collar around his neck.

If you are using a crate to train your puppy, you should remove his collar before shutting him inside, as sadly there have been incidents when collars have become tangled up in the wire mesh of a crate with tragic consequences.

The aim is to teach your Cocker to walk by your side on a loose lead.

Lead training

You can begin lead training as soon as your puppy comes home. Start by attaching a lightweight lead to his collar and let him wander around with it trailing behind him for short periods. Then progress to holding the end of the lead and trying short practice walks in the garden. If your puppy is reluctant to move forwards, it can help to hold a treat out in your other hand to encourage him.

Once your puppy is comfortable wearing a lead, you can start teaching him to walk on a loose lead at your side. This is important because pulling on the lead can be a common problem for Cocker owners and the earlier you teach him not to pull, the better. Cockers have a tendency to pull because their natural exuberance means they are usually very eager to get to where they are going. They quickly realise that pulling works because their owners continue to walk on behind them, i.e. pulling is rewarded by the walk continuing.

The most effective way of training your Cocker not to pull is to never reward this behaviour, meaning that you must stop moving every time he starts to pull. When you stop, your dog will usually turn round to see why he cannot move forward anymore, making the lead slacken. At this moment, you should immediately praise him and then continue walking for as long as the lead remains loose. The process must then be repeated each and every time your dog starts to pull. This stop-start method is generally very effective but it does take considerable patience and persistence, as it can be some time before your Cocker finally gets the message that pulling gets him nowhere.

There are various lead-training aids available, such as anti-pull harnesses and head collars, and while these are undeniably useful, especially in the short-term, they are no substitute for actually putting the work in to train your dog to walk calmly on a loose lead.

If your Cocker attempts to pull, you must come to a complete standstill and not continue until the lead is slack.

Come

The recall is a command every Cocker puppy needs to learn since this is a breed that can have a strong hunting instinct. This means a Cocker can sometimes be more interested in following his nose than listening to his owner. Young puppies are often quite dependent on their owners and reluctant to wander too far from them, so it is the ideal time to start teaching the Come exercise. It becomes much more difficult when a Cocker reaches adolescence and becomes more independent and inclined to be selectively deaf to the owner's calls.

The Come exercise needs to be associated with positive experiences to make your puppy want to return to you from whatever he is doing. You can start teaching your puppy to "Come" in the garden, using tasty

To begin with your puppy will want to follow you, so this is a good time to work on the recall.

The recall should be a really positive exercise so your Cocker wants to come to you.

treats, or a favourite toy if he is not food-motivated, to reward him for responding. You can then progress to practising in other areas with more distractions.

While you are teaching your puppy to come, it can be useful to use a long training line attached to a harness, especially if you do not have access to enclosed exercise areas. This will enable your puppy to have some freedom to explore, but he will still be under your control while he is being trained.

Always use a happy but confident tone of voice and positive body language when calling your pup. For example, bending down and holding your arms out is more inviting to a dog than standing and frowning, with your arms crossed. Never scold your puppy for returning to you, even if he has taken his time to respond to you. Shouting at a Cocker for coming back to you too slowly will guarantee that he will not bother coming at all the next time you call.

Sit

Teaching your puppy to Sit is usually quite easy and takes relatively little time. Start by standing in front of your pup, holding a tasty treat. Then move the treat above your puppy's head and keep moving it slowly backwards. You should find that as your puppy tries to follow the treat with his eyes, his bottom will naturally hit the floor and he will sit, even if only for a second. When he does this, immediately reward him and give him the treat. Repeat this regularly, and when your puppy understands what is expected, you can introduce the verbal cue, "Sit." Eventually the treats can become less frequent, but you should continue to give verbal praise for a good response. Remember to practise in as many different places as possible so that your puppy learns to respond wherever he is.

Stay

Once your puppy has mastered the Sit command, you can then start to teach him the Stay, meaning he must stay where he is until you say he can move. This is useful if you need your dog to stay still while you open a door or have visitors round to the house. This command is more difficult to teach, as it is natural for a Cocker to want to follow you whenever you move away from him, so you will need to be patient and work slowly, a step at a time. It can

With practice, your Cocker will respond to a verbal cue to "Sit".

help to start teaching this command when your pup is slightly tired after a play session or a walk. If he is too excited and bouncy, he is going to find it hard to stay still.

Start by telling your puppy to "Sit" and slowly move one step back from him. Return to him straight away, give him a treat and praise him softly. Do not overdo the

Be patient when teaching the Stay exercise, as a Cocker's natural desire is to follow you.

praise, as you want your pup to remain calm. Repeat this process, but wait a second or two before returning, then progress to moving two steps away. At this stage, you can introduce the verbal command "Stay". Gradually increasing the time you wait before returning to your pup and the number of steps you move away from him. This will take time, so try not to rush things or become frustrated if your puppy cannot seem to stay still for more than a second or two at first.

If your puppy breaks the stay before you come back with the treat, then just go back to the beginning and start again, always aiming to end your training session on a good note. You should start to see steady improvement if you practise this exercise little and often.

Wait

The Wait command is different to the Stay, as the aim is to make him pause briefly before you give another command, e.g. waiting at the side of the road before crossing over or waiting while you open the front door. You will find your Cocker will pick this command up very quickly if you practise your Wait command in a calm, assertive voice at times when he is anticipating something enjoyable, such as a meal or going out for a walk. When you are getting his food bowl ready, give the Sit command and do not put the bowl down until he has waited for a couple of seconds. You can then say, "Okay" – your cue to tell your dog that he can now eat his food. When your puppy understands what is required, introduce the verbal cue "Wait".

Practise this in other situations, such as before you open the door to go out for a walk with your Cocker; his reward for waiting is that the door opens so he can go out for some fun. If he does not wait and tries to barge through, the door is closed again. As with all training, practice sessions need to be kept short but repeated often.

Teaching "No" and "Leave"

"No" is often used by owners to quickly interrupt an unwanted behaviour, such as when your Cocker is chewing something potentially dangerous, but the tone of your voice is more important than the word chosen.

Instead of "No", many owners find that saying something like "Ah ah" in a sharp voice is more effective at getting a dog's attention and stopping him in his tracks. Once you have done this, it is not enough to simply interrupt the behaviour, otherwise he could go straight back to doing it. You need to tell your dog what he should be doing by directing him towards a more positive activity – for example,

There are times when a "Leave" command can be very useful...

offering one of his own safe toys to chew or by doing a short training session.

Teaching your puppy to "Leave" items on command is very important, especially as some Cockers have a tendency to be possessive over things they pick up. If your Cocker picks up an item you do not want him to have, it can be tempting to simply grab him and forcibly try to remove the item from his mouth. Unfortunately, this often has the effect of making a dog defend his 'treasure', making him even more possessive the next time he finds something he wants to keep to himself.

The best way to teach your puppy to leave items on command is to either play a game of swap, where you offer a favourite toy in exchange for the forbidden item, or to use high-value treats – an extra-tasty titbit – so that your Cocker learns that something very enjoyable comes his way if he leaves his 'treasure'.

The Ideal Cocker Owner

The ideal owner knows that the Cocker is not just a pretty face; he is a busy, active dog needing plenty of exercise, human companionship and interesting activities to keep his brain occupied. He is intelligent and eager to learn but he can sometimes be stubborn and quick to take advantage of an over-indulgent owner who treats him like a baby and fails to lay down any boundaries for acceptable behaviour. The ideal owner understands this and provides patient, consistent training from the start, with the aim of building a partnership based on mutual trust and respect. The effort involved will be amply rewarded when you own a happy, confident Cocker that fits well into family life and is a joy to own.

ACTIVITIES FOR COCKERS

The Cocker is a very versatile breed and there are many activities that owners can enjoy with their dogs, whether at a basic fun level or at a more serious competitive level. Here are some of the most popular activities for Cockers.

Showing

Dog shows range from informal Companion Shows through to the more regulated Open and Championship Shows, which are all licensed by the Kennel Club. Companion Shows are fun, local events aimed at raising funds for charity. Entries are taken on the day for a range of Pedigree Classes and Novelty Classes (e.g. Waggiest Tail or Prettiest Puppy). Such shows are ideal for beginners and usually provide a very enjoyable day out for the family. At Open and Championship Shows, Cocker Spaniels have their own classes and entries have to be made in advance with only KC registered dogs eligible to enter. Competition in the Cocker classes can be very strong, particularly at Championship Show level. Because dogs are judged against the Breed Standard, generally only show-type Cockers are seen at the more formal shows, but Working Cockers are often seen at Companion Shows, particularly in the Novelty Classes.

If you are interested in showing your Cocker, you will find ringcraft classes very helpful. Ringcraft classes are run by clubs all over the country and provide ideal opportunities for socialisation and for learning how to stand and move your Cocker for the show ring.

If you have a good specimen of the breed, you may want to get involved in showing.

The Kennel Club Good Citizen Scheme

This is the largest dog training programme in the UK and aims to promote responsible dog ownership and produce dogs which are happy, well-behaved and under the control of their owners. The scheme offers various levels from the basic Puppy Foundation Assessment and Bronze awards, then progressing to the Silver award and finally Gold, the most advanced award.

As well as demonstrating obedience exercises of advancing difficulty, according to the level of the award, owners also have to answer questions about the care of their dogs and their responsibilities as dog owners. Many Cocker owners have taken part in this scheme, gaining a real sense of achievement with each award passed. The scheme also provides a solid foundation for owners interested in moving on to competitive obedience, or to field trial training if you have a working Cocker.

Agility

Canine agility is a fun sport where dogs complete an obstacle course against the clock. Both strains of Cocker can enjoy agility, but dogs and owners need to be fit, as this is a very fast-moving activity. At competition level, speed is important, and, in recent years,

Working Cockers have become very popular agility dogs – they are usually faster than their show cousins.

If you are interested in agility with your Cocker, you will need to find an agility club where you and your dog will be taught the skills needed, but you will not be able to start training

Both show-bred (above) and working Cockers (below) will enjoy the challenge of agility.

until your Cocker is 12 months old, as dogs need to be fully grown. Some owners are happy just to take part in weekly agility training sessions, but if want to take it to a competitive level and enter agility shows, your Cocker needs to be 18 months old and he also has to be formally measured to determine the category he will compete in – Cockers are either Small or Medium.

Working

As the Cocker was developed as a working gundog breed, it can be enormously satisfying to train your dog to fulfil his original function in the field, and your Cocker will enjoy it too. If you want to train your dog to work, you will need to join a gundog club or obtain the services of a one-to-one gundog trainer. Some owners merely enjoy the

You may have ambitions to train your Cocker to compete in field trials.

experience of gundog training, as it enables their dogs to use their natural instincts and exercise their brains and bodies. Others want their dogs to actually work at various levels, from regular shooting in the season to competing in top-level field trials.

While show-type Cockers can enjoy gundog training and become competent working dogs, only working Cockers will have the drive and stamina needed to reach the standard required for high level field trial competitions. So if your ambitions lie in this direction, you will need a Cocker bred from successful working lines rather than a show-type dog.

SUMMARY

The Cocker Spaniel's versatility plays a big part in the breed's popularity today. Whether you want a dog to show, work in the field or take part in sports like agility, there is a Cocker Spaniel for you. However the Cocker's most popular role is

undoubtedly as family companion. His cheerful nature, compact size and good looks makes him the ideal pet for many families. However just like any other dog, a Cocker needs careful socialisation and training with an owner who understands how his mind works and how to get the best from him. If you can offer this, you will have a wonderful companion and a Cocker to be proud of!

Remember, whatever discipline you choose to compete in, you always take the best dog home with you.

Health Care For Cockers

Once you have decided on your veterinary practice it is important to take your new Cocker Spaniel for a health check as soon as possible. This first examination can be the beginning of a long and happy relationship between your Cocker Spaniel and his veterinary surgeon, and it is a good idea for your vet to get to know him from an early age.

Regular 'weigh-ins' and visits to the surgery to pick up medication for worming and treatment of fleas will accustom him to visiting the vet with no adverse experiences. A few dog treats go a long way in making the consulting room a pleasant place! It is also a good idea for you to mimic a clinical examination at home so your Cocker Spaniel is used to having his ears, eyes, mouth and body inspected.

VACCINATION

Vaccination is vital to prevent and control some of the severe viral and bacterial diseases which can be fatal to dogs. Vaccines work by stimulating the body's natural immune response to provide protection should your dog ever be exposed to the disease. This protection is continued each year by annual booster vaccinations. It is important to remember that your Cocker Spaniel should be as fit and healthy as possible to help the vaccine work fully.

Puppies obtain antibodies from their mother's colostrum (first milk) providing immunity to disease for the first few weeks of life. The level of immunity depends on number of antibodies absorbed from the colostrum and how well the mother is protected from certain diseases. Over a period of time, differing for each puppy, these antibodies decrease and from six weeks of age, a puppy will need his first vaccination. The initial vaccination course contains at least two injections, given two to four weeks apart. Contact with unvaccinated dogs or at risk areas should be avoided until full immunity is established.

Microchipping can be carried out at the same time as vaccination. This is where an electronic chip roughly the size of a grain of rice is inserted under the skin ensuring your dog is traceable. The microchipping company hold your details on a central database which means you can be contacted should he ever

Your vet will advise you when to start a vaccination programme.

accidentally become separated from you.

The diseases protected against by standard vaccination protocols are briefly outlined here, but if your Cocker Spaniel is diagnosed with any of the following he should be kept away from other dogs to prevent spread of infection.

- **Distemper:** Caused by the canine distemper virus (CDV).
- **Infectious Canine Hepatitis:** Caused by canine adenovirus-1 (CAV-1).
- **Parvovirus:** Caused by canine parvovirus (CPV) that can survive for months to years in the environment.
- **Leptospirosis:** Caused by two main strains of spirochaete bacteria, *Lepstospira icterohaemorrhagiae* (affects liver) and *L. canicola* (affects kidneys).
- **Kennel Cough:** Caused by multiple viral and bacterial agents and highly infectious.
- **Herpes:** Caused by the canine herpes virus (CHV).

PARASITES

Cocker Spaniels are active working dogs with an interest, and a nose, into everything! This will result in contact with parasites, both internal and external. This is not necessarily a serious issue if they are adequately controlled. There are several types of worms, the most common being the roundworm. Infection often occurs from eating infected faeces or meat or via an intermediate host.

Treatment in most cases requires worming medication to remove the infection and ongoing preventative medication to prevent build up. All medication should be discussed with your veterinary surgeon for timing, frequency and preparation of wormer. Strict hygiene, especially with faeces, should always be observed.

A dog will behave like a dog – and you have little control over what he comes into contact with.

Roundworms

Toxocara cani: This is a large, round, white worm found in the small intestine. Signs of infection are a pot-belly, occasional diarrhoea or vomiting, poor growth, lethargy, coughing, pneumonia, nasal discharge and even death in young pups with very heavy infections. Regular worming of pups and mother during the early periods of the puppies' lives will prevent severe infections. Adult dogs should be treated every three to six months throughout their lives. It is important to note that this worm can infect humans, most commonly children in contact with dog faeces, potentially resulting in liver damage or blindness.
Toxascaris leonine: Infection occurs via direct ingestion of the egg or as larvae in the tissues of mice and are almost always concurrent with *T. canis* therefore clinical signs and treatment regimes are similar.

Whipworms

Trichuris vulpis: Whipworms have a thick tail and a thin head, hence the name. Light infections often cause no signs but if heavy burdens are present, watery diarrhoea often with blood and mucus present may be seen.

Fleas

Ctenocephalides canis and *C. felis* (more common): The flea is a small, wingless insect with a laterally flattened body and biting mouthparts enabling it to feed on blood. Adults live on the host, and the resulting hundreds of eggs, larvae and pupae are found in the environment. Both species are part of the lifecycle of the common tapeworm of dogs *D. caninum.* When the flea bites, it causes irritation to the skin which results in pruritis (itching) and

A preventative worming programme is essential if your Cocker comes into contact with children.

Tapeworms

Dipylidium caninum: This is the most common of the tapeworm species in the UK. Infection occurs via ingestion of fleas and lice carrying the intermediate lifestage of the worm. The adult worms live in the small intestine and release proglottids (mobile segments containing the eggs) into the faeces. The adults rarely cause clinical disease, although irritation of the anus may be seen as the proglottids emerge. Treatment and control are integral, with insecticide treatment preventing the completion of the lifecycle, whilst regular worming medication removes the adult worms.

Taenia species. (T. multiceps, T. hydatigena, T. ovis, T. pisiformis, T. serialis): Infection occurs via ingestion of infected meat of the intermediate hosts (sheep, rabbits, rodents). These worms are often not of clinical significance in the dog, but are far more important in the intermediate hosts where they can be fatal. Prevention of access to infected meat and regular worming medication controls infection.

Spot on treatment is effective in preventing flea infestation.

inflammation. Regular flea insecticide treatment is required on the dog and good hygiene and aerosol treatment in the environment to help break the lifecycle and reduce numbers.

Ticks

The common types of tick found on dogs in the UK are the *Ixodes ricinus* (sheep tick) and the *I. hexagonus* (hedgehog tick). They are blood

Echinococcus granulosus: This tapeworm is found in the small intestine in dogs, and as larvae in the liver or lungs of the intermediate host (ruminants, man or pig). Large infections are often no issue in the dog. If man is the intermediate host, this may be more severe with clinical signs relating to the larvae forming potentially fatal cysts in the lungs or liver.

Angiostrongylus vasorum: Commonly known as 'lungworm', this parasite lives in the heart and lungs of dogs and foxes and can cause serious illness and even death in affected animals. Once rare in the UK, it is becoming more common particularly in the South of England. The parasite is transmitted from dog and fox faeces to slugs and snails.

Dogs are then infected by eating infected slugs and snails. Many Cockers will try to eat slugs and snails, given the opportunity, so it is important to always supervise your dog when he is outside. You should also be aware of the symptoms of lungworm infection, such as a persistent cough and breathing difficulties. Ask your vet's advice on the most suitable wormer for your Cocker if you know he is a snail-eater as not all worming preparations are effective against lungworm.

sucking parasites which can transmit diseases such as Lyme disease (to both dogs and humans) and Erlichiosis. Bean shaped, they vary in size from 2-10mm and are most commonly found on dogs in spring and autumn. As they feed they swell in size and heavy infestations can cause anaemia. Once the female has mated, she feeds and then drops off the host to lay thousands of eggs.

They can be removed by clockwise rotation of the body, but take care not to leave the mouthparts as infection can occur.

Lice

Lice are highly host specific and unable to survive for long when off the host body. Dogs are hosts to two types of louse, *Linognathus* and *Trichodectes* (a carrier of the

Ringworm/ Dermatophytosis

Microsporum canis is responsible for the majority of ringworm cases with Trichophyton mentagrophytes and Microsporum gypseum also seen. Typically, circular lesions are present with skin scaling and hair loss noted. Topical treatment is used and if infection is severe antibiotics may also be needed.

tapeworm *D. caninum*). Infection results in irritation and skin damage and severe infestations may cause anaemia. Prescription shampoo is often suitable to eliminate infection.

Mites

Otodectes cyanotic: This mite is found in the external ear canal and causes production of a brown, waxy discharge resulting in head shaking, discomfort and pruritis. It can be transmitted by close contact. Infection can be cleared by cleaning the ear canal and applying medicated drops, but if left untreated, secondary infection may occur. This can cause ear drum rupture resulting in deafness and neurological signs, and may prove difficult to treat.

Cheyletiella yasguri: This mite is visible with the naked eye and is often referred to as "walking dandruff". It is a non-burrowing mite that causes pruritis, scaling and scabs on the skin. Treatment is available and effective. Care must be taken as this parasite is zoonotic (transferable to humans).

Demodex canis: This cigar-shaped burrowing mite is found in small numbers on healthy dogs, but disease can occur if the immune system is compromised. Transmission occurs between mother and pups while feeding, and infection is often seen in young dogs with scaling, hair loss, pustules and skin infections especially around the face. Occasionally the feet may be affected. Treatment involves repeated applications of topical medication and occasionally antibiotics.

Sarcoptes scabiei: This highly contagious burrowing mite causes intense pruritis around the ears, muzzle, face and elbows and, if severe, all over the body. Clinical signs involve pustules, crust formation, alopecia and there may be self trauma from itching. Treatment requires repeated bathing with a medicated shampoo, with isolation until eliminated to prevent transmission.

A-Z OF COMMON AILMENTS

Anal gland disorders
Anal glands are small sacs that empty into the anus when defecation occurs. They produce a dark-brown, pungent liquid which is used by dogs to mark their territory. Occasionally they may become blocked or impacted causing irritation, causing your Cocker Spaniel to drag his bottom along the floor (scooting), have problems toileting or nibble around the tail area.

At this point they can be manually expressed to clear the blockage. If the blockage is not cleared then infection may occur and form an abscess within the gland. This will need veterinary attention.

Factors that may play a part in causing impaction are diarrhoea, soft faeces and obesity. Cocker Spaniels seem to be prone to anal gland problems and persistent recurrence may eventually require surgery to remove the affected gland completely.

Dental problems
Periodontal disease is the most common oral disease in dogs, and Cocker Spaniels are no exception. Tartar can be seen as young as nine months of age and is normally first noticed on the upper back teeth, spreading and getting worse over time. Your dog's teeth should be examined regularly to assess the level of disease and decide whether treatment is necessary.

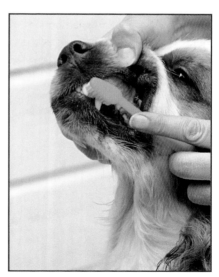

Tooth brushing from an early age should help prevent dental problems.

Initially plaque (soft debris, bacteria and staining) deposits on the teeth which over time, mineralises and forms tartar. Once tartar is present, it spreads under the gums causing pain and inflammation (gingivitis) seen as reddening of the gums. The bacteria in the tartar can enter the bloodstream, due to the increased blood supply which occurs during the inflammatory process, and be carried to the organs (e.g. liver, kidneys), resulting in infection. Severe tartar causes gum recession, root exposure and loss of teeth.

Minimal deposit on the teeth can be controlled with a healthy diet, tooth brushing and dental chews. Tooth brushing should be taught at an early age – prevention is better than cure!

Once tartar has formed, this cannot be removed by brushing and will only become worse with time. At this point, an anaesthetic may be needed to remove the tartar manually. The condition of the teeth beneath the tartar, determines whether or not they need extracting. After dentistry, it is very important to maintain dental health and it may be advisable to alter the diet to encompass your dog's dental requirements.

Diabetes

Diabetes Mellitus (DM) is one of the most common endocrine disorders encountered, most often seen in middle aged, overweight dogs. Glucose is absorbed by cells in the presence of insulin, and is the energy source for cell survival.

DM occurs when insulin production (by the pancreas) is inadequate or the body's cells fail to respond to insulin properly. This results in an inability to absorb the glucose causing high blood levels and subsequently glucose in the urine. The most common clinical signs are excessive drinking and urination, increased appetite and weight loss, although coat changes and lethargy may also occur. If left untreated, it can

The onset of diabetes is usually seen in middle-aged dogs.

progress to blindness caused by cataracts or further to a diabetic coma. Treatment is comparable to humans with daily insulin injections for life.

Ear infections

The ear is made up of three different sections:

- **The external ear:** This includes the pinna (earflap) and the ear canal extending as far as the tympanic membrane (ear drum).
- **The middle ear:** This is an air filled cavity that contains three small bones which vibrate and transmit the sound to the inner ear.
- **The inner ear:** This is a fluid filled cavity which contains the cochlea (organ for hearing) and the vestibular apparatus (organ involved in balance).

Infection can occur commonly in the outer ear (**otitis externa**) resulting in a brown, waxy discharge, often accompanied with a characteristic smell and reddening of the skin. This will cause your dog to shake his head or scratch at his ears in response to the irritation. If the infection spreads deeper into the middle ear (**otitis media**) or inner ear (**otitis interna**) then this may cause neurological signs such as lack of co-ordination, imbalance, circling or a head tilt.

Cocker Spaniels can be susceptible to ear infections and irritations due to their long pinnae, the narrowness

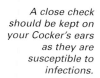

A close check should be kept on your Cocker's ears as they are susceptible to infections.

of the ear canal in some dogs, and their love of water. Regular grooming and trimming of the hair inside the ear flap will help to maintain healthy ears. Occasionally foreign bodies (e.g. grass seeds) can enter the ear canal and remain there. Ear mites (see page 108) cause irritation and wax production. Bacteria and yeasts can enter the ear and when growth becomes uncontrolled infection occurs.

Treatment involves clearing any infection and removing excess wax. There are many topical preparations available but if infection is severe or non-responsive, investigation under anaesthetic may be required to flush the ear canal. If left untreated, the ear may become impacted, the skin may become thickened from chronic inflammation and ultimately surgery may be the only option.

Eye disorders

Eyelids: The eyelids cover and protect the delicate structures of the eye and ensure that the outer surface remains clean and lubricated. Cocker Spaniels can suffer from both **entropion** (inward rotation) and **ectropion** (outward

Eyes should be clear, bright and sparkling, with no hint of discharge, redness or inflammation.

The Cocker is a breed that exercises with nose to ground, so his eyes can be vulnerable if he is working through undergrowth.

rotation) of the eyelids which may result in inflammation and infection. Occasionally the tear ducts may not develop correctly causing the eyes to overflow with tears. Hairs from the periocular area may deviate (**trichiasis**) and eyelashes may grow in the wrong direction (**distichiasis**) causing irritation to the eye. If causing a problem these hairs can be removed to prevent more severe damage. Small, wart-like growths on the lids may occur, which is not usually a problem unless they grow large or touch the cornea causing trauma. Cocker Spaniels do appear to be predisposed to limbal melanomas – a type of tumour, often pigmented, of the area around the edge of the cornea. Removal is often curative.

Lens: The lens is found behind the pupil and focuses light rays so that objects can be seen clearly.
Cataracts are an opacification (blue-whitening) of the lens progressively resulting in impaired vision, not to be

confused with **nuclear sclerosis** (grey-blue haze) which occurs in older animals and doesn't cause blindness.

Retina: The retina is the layer at the back of the eye that receives light rays and is composed of cells called rods and cones. Rods aid vision in low light and cones help determine different colours; dogs eyes are especially plentiful in rods compared to humans hence better in lower light levels but not in colour. Cocker Spaniels can suffer from retinal disease (see Hereditary Disorders).

Cornea: The cornea is the transparent layer at the front of the eye that allows light to enter. With their inherent need to work every bit of undergrowth, Cocker Spaniels may occasionally damage the cornea. **Trauma** to the cornea can result in tear production, blinking and pain, and if untreated may progress to infection and ulceration. **Ulceration** is where some of the cornea is damaged, often accompanied by conjunctivitis. If superficial then this may be treated with medicated eye drops but if the injury persists or the initial ulcer is deeper, then there is a risk of rupture of the eye.

Conjunctivitis is the term for inflammation, discomfort and reddening of the conjunctiva (tissues around the eye). There are many causes of conjunctivitis from bacterial and viral to trauma. Any sign of conjunctivitis could potentially be serious and requires veterinary attention. **Dry Eye** is the term applied to an inadequate tear film and drying of the conjunctiva and cornea. Cocker Spaniels appear predisposed to this disorder and as a result may have an increased incidence of infection and ulceration of the cornea. Treatment is usually in the form of lifelong artificial tears.

Gastrointestinal disorders

Foreign Bodies: All dogs like to play with toys (and what they think are their toys but in fact are the family heirloom!) and to feel the sensation of new substances with their mouths. If swallowed, the intestine may become either partially or completely obstructed. Blockages in the intestinal tract can result in anorexia, vomiting, abdominal pain or diarrhoea. The degree of severity of clinical signs usually depends on the degree and duration of obstruction. If a blockage has occurred, the only option is surgery to remove the obstruction.

Intestinal Intussusception: This is where the intestine folds in on itself, often caused by hypermotility (excessive gut movement), to form a double tube which constricts causing obstruction. Obstruction may initially be partial and proceed to complete. This condition is more common in young dogs (six to eight months) with clinical signs being vomiting, abdominal pain, anorexia and diarrhoea, occasionally with blood.

Watch out for your puppy – or adult – chewing a toy and then swallowing part of it.

Surgery is needed to remove any damaged intestine.

Gastritis: This is inflammation of the stomach lining typically resulting in vomiting. There are multiple causes, with scavenging usually high on the list of probabilities. Vomiting is the body's natural defence against poisoning and occasionally dogs may eat grass to bring on vomiting if they feel nauseous. Single episodes of vomiting are often seen and are not a problem in the dog as long as he remains bright and well. If vomiting continues or your dog appears unwell, a trip to the vet will be needed.

Diarrhoea: There are many reasons for diarrhoea. Often frequency of defecation increases and there may be blood or mucus present. Sometimes a simple 24 hour withdrawal of food can be enough to help clear any upset. At other times the condition can be life threatening. If your Cocker Spaniel is unwell or off colour; if he is vomiting, or blood is noted in the faeces, veterinary advice should be sought.

Common cuases of diarrhoea

Dietary: Any dog owner will know that all dogs at some point eat something that would not normally be considered on a menu! Rubbish

The Cocker can be hypersensitive to some foods, so you will need to monitor his diet in order to avoid diarrhoea.

bins which can be raided by your Cocker Spaniel, may contain unsavoury and potentially poisonous items. Therefore, bins inside and outside the house should be well secured. Sudden diet changes can upset the normal intestinal microflora so any diet alteration should be carried out over a four to five day period, gradually increasing the amount of the new diet. Hypersensitivities to food can be seen in the Cocker Spaniel (often with concurrent skin or ear problems) resulting in chronic diarrhoea, and it can be a frustrating condition to diagnose involving diet trials with specially formulated feedstuffs.

Bacterial infections (Salmonella, Campylobacter, E. coli): Care needs to be taken if these have been diagnosed, as they are potentially transmissible to humans so strict hygiene methods should be employed to minimise the risks. Antibiotics are the mainstay of treatment, but severe cases may need hospitalisation.

Viral infections (Canine Distemper, Canine Parvovirus, Coronavirus): These often require supportive treatment as there is rarely antiviral therapy available.

Parasites: A heavy worm burden may result in diarrhoea, and a regular worming regime should be employed to prevent them being a possible cause of any upset.

Enteritis: This is inflammation of the small intestine and again there is a long list of potential causes. Diarrhoea in large volumes with minimal straining occurs and may be seen with abdominal pain, dehydration, vomiting, anorexia and weight loss. Treatment is dependent on the cause, severity and duration of the disease.

Colitis: This is inflammation of the colon and can have multiple causes. Often diarrhoea is seen which may be watery in consistency with either blood or mucus or both present. Repeated attempts to pass faeces are

Hypothyroidism

This is a common endocrine disease where there is an underproduction of thyroxine (hormone controlling metabolic rate of the body) from the thyroid gland. Generally seen in middle aged dogs of larger breeds but the Cocker Spaniel may be at an increased risk. The low levels result in weakness, lethargy, reduced body temperature, weight gain, slow heart rate, hair loss, weight gain and skin problems. Treatment, often successful, is in the form of an oral synthetic hormone.

seen, with straining, often only producing small volumes. Treatment is dependant on the cause, severity and duration of disease.

Joint disorders

The bones and joints of all dogs are sensitive to physical trauma and disease, and even with four legs they occasionally manage to lose their footing and trip! Cocker Spaniels are active, bouncy dogs and will keep working until they (or you!) drop… which may occasionally result in trauma to the joints.

Initial clinical signs that there may be a problem are lameness, stiffness and pain on movement. Usually a full physical examination and X-rays are necessary to help diagnose the problem. Any trauma to a joint will result in an increased susceptibility of that joint to succumb to arthritis later in life.

Osteoarthritis (OA): This degenerative joint disease results in the joints becoming enlarged, painful and stiff. Often seen in the older Cocker Spaniel, the first signs may be stiffness and slight lameness especially after longer walks which progress to a reluctance to exercise and severe lameness. There are many joint supplements and diets available to help slow progression of the disease, and pain relieving medications to make your dog more comfortable in more severe cases. Ensuring that your Cocker Spaniel does not put on weight in later years will reduce the load on the joints.

Hip Dysplasia (HD): See Inherited Disorders.

Osteochodrosis and Osteochondritis Dissecans (OCD): This is inflammation and pain of the bone and cartilage, often due to abnormalities or trauma, and the ensuing damage resulting in a flap of cartilage breaking off into the joint (joint mouse). Occasionally seen in the young, growing Cocker Spaniel, this can be very painful, especially if

A regime of regular exercise matched with a balanced diet will help to prevent obesity.

the fragment moves within the joint, and surgery may be needed to remove it.

Cruciate rupture: The cruciate ligaments of the stifle (knee) can be partially or completely torn when placed under significant physical stress resulting in lameness. Treatment often involves surgery along with an extended period of rest. The affected joint is prone to arthritis later in life.

Obesity

Physical fitness is a very important aspect of your dog's routine healthcare. Cocker Spaniels enjoy exercise and will work all day, but generally they tend to put on weight with age and a corresponding reduction in exercise. Obesity can have concerning medical effects, and with more dogs nowadays being overweight, a corresponding increase in weight related medical problems are also being noted.

A high body fat percentage increases anaesthetic and surgical risks. With increased body weight, there is more physical stress placed on the muscles, bones and joints and this can result in severe arthritis and joint problems in later life.

Increased amounts of fat are also deposited around the internal organs, as in humans, and result in reduced function or dysfunction. Other medical diseases include diabetes, heart disease and breathing problems.

Regular exercise and a healthy diet from the start are the magic ingredients to a fit and healthy dog. Treats can be high in fats and sugars, and should not be given on a regular basis. Using part of the daily diet ration is a good way to treat without increasing the calorific intake. Human food is often unsuitable for dogs and may be poisonous, so take care when giving scraps from your plate. There are specially formulated diets available to help with weight loss but they need to be used together with increased exercise and a strict no treats regime.

Skin conditions

Cocker Spaniels as a breed tend to have a full, silky coat and healthy skin. There are, however, a few conditions which can affect them.

Atopy: This is an inherited predisposition to develop a hypersensitivity to environmental allergens (e.g. pollens, dust mites, moulds). Initial signs are licking, itching and reddening of skin, which may progress to self trauma, secondary infection, scaling and crusting. Treatment can involve steroids, antibiotics and even desensitisation vaccines following testing to determine the allergen.

Food Hypersensitivity: Cocker Spaniels can also have reactions to allergens in food. This may result in chronic diarrhoea, intolerance of certain foods, itchy skin or sore ears. The clinical signs are often variable in severity and diagnosis involves lengthy and strict food trials.

Intertrigo: This is where the skin rubs becoming red and moist, with an increased likelihood of developing infection. Cocker Spaniels often suffer this in the folds of skin around the lips. Very often, the first sign that your Cocker is suffering from a lip fold infection will be an extremely unpleasant smell although it is not always easy to tell just where the smell is coming from! Useful preventative measures include keeping the hair in the lip fold area clipped as short as possible, and

Interdigital Dermatitis

Cocker Spaniels can suffer from irritated skin between their toes due to the large number of hairs growing there. This can lead to excessive licking, skin trauma and infection. They may also get grass seeds penetrating the skin around the toes which can migrate up the leg becoming very painful and infected. Bathing and antibiotics are usually sufficient to keep infection under control, although surgery may be required to remove the offending grass seed.

patting the area dry after eating and drinking; moist conditions increase the risk of infection. Cleansing shampoos will also help to keep skin dry but antibiotics may be needed if infection occurs. In severe cases, surgical removal of the lip fold is usually very successful.

Tumours: Cocker Spaniels do tend to suffer from some skin tumours as they get older. Commonly this takes the form of benign masses but, unfortunately, the Cocker may also be predisposed to some malignant tumours. Any lumps or bumps that you notice should be examined by your

Urinary Conditions

Urine is produced in the kidneys (by filtering blood), transported via the ureters (tubes) to the bladder, where it is stored before being passed through the urethra (a tube) to the penis or vagina and voided. Any abnormality of urine or the act of urination can indicate a problem at any point of the urinary tract. Your Cocker Spaniel should always have free access to fresh water at all times to help reduce the risk of problems.

Clinical signs are often similar irrespective of the cause. Look for straining or repeated attempts to pass urine; difficult, slow or painful urination; incontinence and abnormally strong smelling or dark coloured urine. If you notice any of these then, if possible, collect a fresh sample in a clean glass jar and take it with you to the veterinary surgery so they can analyse it after examining your dog.

A few of the common problems are listed below:

Bacterial cystitis: This is a bacterial infection in the bladder and is more commonly, but not exclusively, seen in bitches. Older, Cocker Spaniel females appear to be prone and often antibiotics are indicated to help clear the infection.

Bladder stones (uroliths): These are stones formed within the bladder and although small to start with, may become very large. Factors

veterinary surgeon who may advise taking a sample to be checked by a pathologist to determine treatment.

MISCELLANEOUS

Rage syndrome

Mention is often made of cases of sudden uncharacteristic aggression once seen in Cockers (primarily in the solid colours but not exclusively), and in numerous other breeds, which became widely known as rage syndrome. An affected dog would suffer sudden, unpredictable bursts of severe aggression, during which he

affecting formation of uroliths are diet, water intake, breed and urinary tract infection. There are different types of stone which need to be identified to ensure correct treatment. Cocker Spaniels have been noted to be susceptible to struvite and calcium phosphate uroliths, although still uncommon. If left untreated they may have potentially life-threatening consequences by blocking the urethra thereby preventing passage of urine. Stones may also form in the kidneys causing severe abdominal pain whilst passing through the ureters.

Renal failure: Kidneys can become damaged by infections, toxins or degenerate due to old age resulting in reduced working capacity. Clinical signs are not obviously noticeable until more than three-quarters of the functioning tissue is affected. Early signs of kidney failure are drinking more and production of large volumes of dilute urine. As the disease progresses vomiting, loss of appetite and lethargy are commonly noted. There is an inherited form of renal failure (See Inherited Disorders).

Tumours: Growths can occur in the bladder and cause problems with obstructing the flow of urine.

Incontinence: This is an inability to control the act of urination and can have many contributing factors such as infections, tumours and old age affecting the ability of urine retention.

would not appear to know what he was doing and then return just as quickly to normal.

The cause of this condition has never been conclusively established, although a number of theories have been suggested, such as it being a type of epilepsy. However, true cases of rage syndrome are now rare and most cases of aggression involving a Cocker are due to other causes (health issues, lack of training, poor handling etc).

If you are worried your Cocker is suffering from rage syndrome, first consult your vet for a full examination to rule out a physical health problem and if all is well, seek the advice of an experienced, qualified behaviourist.

INHERITED AND BREED-DISPOSED DISORDERS

The Cocker Spaniel does have a few breed related disorders, and if a Cocker is diagnosed with any of the diseases listed below, it is important to remember that they can affect offspring so breeding from affected dogs should be strongly discouraged.

The British Veterinary Association (BVA), the Kennel Club (KC) and the International Sheep Dog Society (ISDS) have set up various screening

Immune-mediated Haemolytic Anaemia

This is a condition where the body's immune system sees the red blood cells in the bloodstream as foreign and destroys them. Cocker Spaniels appear to have a predisposition to this disease. Presentation of clinical signs can vary from mild to severe anaemia with chronic to acute onset and life threatening collapse due to reduced oxygen carrying capacity of the blood. Often this may be managed medically with immuno-suppressive medications but if severe repeated blood transfusions may be necessary.

tests to enable breeders to check for affected individuals and hence reduce the prevalence of these diseases within the breed.

All breeding stock should be health checked to help eliminate inherited conditions.

Generalised Progressive Retinal Atrophy (GPRA)

GPRA is a bilateral degenerative disease of the retina leading initially to night blindness and progressing to complete loss of vision. There may be some association with cataract formation. Clinical identification is by examination of the eye, and the BVA/CK/ISDS Eye Scheme aims to identify affected individuals.

There is also a DNA test available for the most commonly seen form of GPRA in Cockers, known as prcd_PRA. A simple blood sample or cheek swab can be tested to determine whether a dog is Normal (Clear), a Carrier of the condition or Affected. Carrier dogs will never develop the disease but can produce affected dogs if mated to other carriers. The DNA test means that breeders can identify carriers before breeding and so can now avoid breeding affected dogs.

Hip dysplasia

This is where the ball and socket joint of the hip develops incorrectly so that the head of the femur (ball) and the acetabulum of the pelvis (socket) do not fit snugly. This results in joint pain and may cause lameness in dogs as young as 5 months with deterioration into severe arthritis over time. Cocker Spaniels, like many other breeds, can be affected with HD. The BVA/KC HD Scheme available involves your veterinary surgeon taking x-rays and sending them to the BVA where a "hip score" is allocated determining the severity of disease.

Retinal Pigment Epithelial Dystrophy (RPED)

RPED, previously called Centralised Progressive Retinal Atrophy (CPRA), is where an accumulation of pigment occurs in the retina resulting in a slowly progressive loss of vision. There may be some link between RPED and vitamin E deficiency, and supplementation may prove helpful in preventing progression of the disease.

There is a BVA/KC/ISDS Eye Scheme available for this condition, determined by an eye examination.

Goniodysgenesis/primary glaucoma

This is where there is abnormal development of the eye so that fluid that is constantly being produced within the eye (aqueous humour) cannot drain adequately. This over time results in an increase in pressure within the eye and clinical signs of acute redness and pain. Medication alone is not usually enough to treat and surgery is often indicated to relieve the pressure. Predisposition to Glaucoma can be tested for under the BVA/KC/ISDS Eye Scheme (Gonioscopy test).

Familial nephropathy

This disease affects Cocker Spaniels from the age of six months to two years. It is believed to be damage to the glomerular basement membrane in the kidney which causes fatal renal failure. It used to be more prevalent, but breeding schemes have reduced the incidence dramatically, and nowadays it is rarely seen.

A DNA test is also now available meaning carriers of this condition can be identified prior to breeding. As with prcd_PRA, FN Carriers will never develop the disease but can produce affected dogs if mated to other carriers. The DNA test means that breeders can identify carriers before breeding and so can now avoid breeding affected dogs

SUMMING UP

It may give the pet owner cause for concern to find about health problems that may affect their dog. But it is important to bear in mind that acquiring some basic knowledge is an asset as it will allow you to spot signs of trouble at an early stage. Early diagnosis is very often the means to the most effective treatment.

Fortunately the Cocker Spaniel is a generally healthy and disease free dog, and in most cases, owners can look forward to enjoying many happy years with this happy-go-lucky, bustling friend.

With good care and management, your Cocker should live a long life and suffer few health problems.

Useful Addresses

BREED CLUBS
Please contact the Kennel Club to obtain contact information about breed clubs in your area.

KENNEL CLUBS
American Kennel Club (AKC)
5580 Centerview Drive, Raleigh, NC 27606.
Telephone: 919 233 9767
Fax: 919 233 3627
Email: info@akc.org
Web: www.akc.org

The Kennel Club (UK)
1 Clarges Street London, W1J 8AB
Telephone: 0870 606 6750
Fax: 0207 518 1058
Web: www.thekennelclub.org.uk

TRAINING AND BEHAVIOUR
Association of Pet Dog Trainers (APDT)
PO Box 17, Kempsford, GL7 4WZ
Telephone: 01285 810811
Email: APDToffice@aol.com
Web: http://www.apdt.co.uk

Association of Pet Behaviour Counsellors (APBC)
PO BOX 46, Worcester, WR8 9YS
Telephone: 01386 751151
Fax: 01386 750743
Email: info@apbc.org.uk
Web: http://www.apbc.org.uk/

ACTIVITIES
Agility Club
http://www.agilityclub.co.uk/

British Flyball Association
PO Box 990, Doncaster, DN1 9FY
Telephone: 01628 829623
Email: secretary@flyball.org.uk
Web: http://www.flyball.org.uk/

World Canine Freestyle Organisation
P.O. Box 350122, Brooklyn, NY 11235-2525
Telephone: 718 332-8336
Fax: 718 646-2686
Email: wcfodogs@aol.com
Web: www.worldcaninefreestyle.org

HEALTH
Alternative Veterinary Medicine Centre
Chinham House, Stanford in the Vale, Oxon, SN7 8NQ
Telephone: 01367 710324
Fax: 01367 718243
Web: www.alternativevet.org/

Animal Health Trust
Lanwades Park, Kentford, Newmarket, Suffolk, CB8 7UU
Telephone: 01638 751000
Website: www.aht.org.uk

British Association of Veterinary Ophthalmologists (BAVO)
Email: secretary@bravo.org.uk
Web: http://www.bravo.org.uk/

British Small Animal Veterinary Association (BSAVA)
Woodrow House, 1 Telford Way, Waterwells Business Park, Quedgeley, Gloucestershire, GL2 2AB
Telephone: 01452 726700
Fax: 01452 726701
Email: customerservices@bsava.com
Web: http://www.bsava.com/

British Veterinary Hospitals Association (BHVA)
Station Bungalow, Main Rd, Stocksfield,
Northumberland, NE43 7HJ
Telephone: 07966 901619
Fax: 07813 915954
Email: office@bvha.org.uk
Web: http://www.bvha.org.uk/

Royal College of Veterinary Surgeons (RCVS)
Belgravia House, 62-64 Horseferry Road, London, SW1P 2AF
Telephone: 0207 222 2001
Fax: 0207 222 2004
Email: admin@rcvs.org.uk
Web: www.rcvs.org.uk

ASSISTANCE DOGS
Canine Partners
Mill Lane, Heyshott, Midhurst, West Sussex, GU29 0ED
Telephone: 08456 580480
Fax: 08456 580481
www.caninepartners.co.uk

Dogs for the Disabled
The Frances Hay Centre, Blacklocks Hill, Banbury, Oxon, OX17 2BS
Telephone: 01295 252600
Web: www.dogsforthedisabled.org

Guide Dogs for the Blind Association
Burghfield Common, Reading, Berkshire, RG7 3YG
Telephone: 0118 983 5555
Fax: 0118 983 5433
Web: www.guidedogs.org.uk/

Hearing Dogs for Deaf People
The Grange, Wycombe Road, Saunderton, Princes Risborough,
Bucks, HP27 9NS
Telephone: 01844 348100
Fax: 01844 348101
Web: hearingdogs.org.uk

Pets as Therapy
3a Grange Farm Cottages, Wycombe Road,
Saunderton, Princes Risborough, Bucks, HP27 9NS
Telephone: 01845 345445
Fax: 01845 550236
Web: http://www.petsastherapy.org/

Support Dogs
21 Jessops Riverside, Brightside Lane, Sheffield, S9 2RX
Tel: 01142 617800
Fax: 01142 617555
Email: supportdogs@btconnect.com
Web: www.support-dogs.org.uk

About The Authors

JANE SIMMONDS (SHENMORE)
Jane has owned Cocker Spaniels, together with her husband Andrew, for 25 years. Like many others, they started off with one pet Cocker which then developed into a lifelong passion for the breed. They breed occasionally under the Shenmore affix and show their dogs with some success (having made up three Show Champions as well owning several other CC winners). Jane is an approved judge of Cocker Spaniels at Championship Show level and is also an experienced groomer.

Jane has a particular interest in health issues affecting Cockers and works to promote responsible breeding using the available health tests (she and her husband were the first UK breeders to use the DNA test for the eye disease PRA when it became available). She also fosters rescue Cockers from time to time and helps run a busy internet forum for owners of Cocker Spaniels which provides help and advice on all aspects of living with this lovely breed.

ESTELA BADEN **BSc Hons BVSc MRCVS**
Estela graduated as a veterinary surgeon from Liverpool University in 2006. Since qualifying she has been working in a small animal practice in Monmouthshire. Whilst interested in all aspects of small animal practice, she has particular interests in small animal surgery and animal behaviour.
See Chapter Six: Health Care for Cockers.

Further Reading

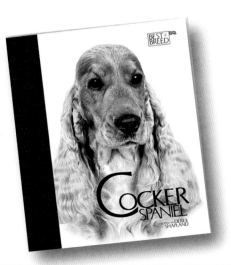

Cocker Spaniel
(BEST OF BREED)

Written by leading British experts, including Derek Shapland, *The Cocker Spaniel* offers readers an unrivalled depth of knowledge about their chosen breed. The book gives detailed information on character and behaviour, puppy care, training and socialisation, with a special chapter on Cocker health written by a leading British vet. Illustrated by a stunning collection of more than 120 specially-commissioned colour photographs, matched by the high-specification production, and distinctively finished with real cloth binding, this is one breed book no Cocker lover should be without.

Available in the UK from Corpus Publishing,
St Martin's Farm, Zeals, Warminster, BA12 6NP, UK.
Price: £14.99 (plus £2 p+p)

Index